MY NAKBA

A Palestinian's Odyssey of Love and Hope

by Samir Toubassy

OLIVE
BRANCH
PRESS

An imprint of Interlink Publishing Group, Inc.
www.interlinkbooks.com

First published in 2019 by

Olive Branch Press
An imprint of Interlink Publishing Group, Inc.
46 Crosby Street, Northampton, MA 01060
www.interlinkbooks.com

Copyright © Samir Toubassy, 2019
Cover photograph: Background Pastel Chalk Crayon Abstract ©
LazingBee I istockphoto

Author's note: this book is based on my personal recollection, and
any errors, omissions, or misrepresentations are my own.

All rights reserved; no part of this publication may be reproduced,
stored in a retrieval system, or transmitted, in any form or by any
means, electronic, mechanical, photocopying, recording or otherwise,
without the prior written permission of the publisher.

Library of Congress Cataloging-in-Publication Data
Names: Toubassy, Samir, 1939– author.
Title: My Nakba: a Palestinian's odyssey of love and hope / by Samir
    Toubassy.
Description: Northampton, MA : Olive Branch Press, an imprint of
    Interlink Publishing Group, Inc., [2019]
Identifiers: LCCN 2019012627
Subjects: LCSH: Toubassy, Samir, 1939– I Refugees, Palestinian
    Arab—Biography. I Investment advisors—Biography. I Olayan
    Group—Biography. I Israel-Arab War, 1948-1949—Refugees.
Classification: LCC HV640.5.P36 T596 2019 I DDC 956.04/21
    [B]—dc23
LC record available at https://lccn.loc.gov/2019012627

Printed and bound in the United States of America

Cochrane
Marigold Library System

-- JUL 2019

MY NAKBA

*"Tell me the landscape where you live,
and I will tell you who you are."*
—José Ortega y Gasset

Preface

The expulsion of Palestinians from our homeland in 1948, the *Nakba*, meaning *disaster* or *catastrophe*, was a turning point in our history. It was lived and is remembered in many ways by different Palestinians.

Throughout my life, my experience of the Nakba has been a constant shadow. It has always been with me, nagging at me, reminding me of others, raising doubts, questioning my choices. One lesson I've taken to heart from this shadow is that being a victim is not, and could never be, an identity.

Being targeted or victimized is a condition that we may suffer, but one that can never define who we are. "Refugee" is an imposed status that covers up a person's true identity, potential and dignity.

From my family, culture and my faith, I learned that we are all children of the Creator and members of a human family. Strengthening my resolve to define myself through my actions, this made me ask how I might achieve something in the world, while holding onto my values and trying to make a difference.

Beyond that, it led me to see family in larger ways, to identify with other people's disasters and try to do something about them, to understand my own story as one small piece of a bigger puzzle.

My Nakba is where 1948 led me.

—Samir Toubassy, 2019

I

1
LEAVING JAFFA

In the spring of 1948, when I was nine years old, my parents woke us up very early one morning. All I could think about was the scent of orange blossoms. Winter was ending, and nature was sending out its first fragrant signs of spring. But my parents faced a more urgent task than enjoying the orange blossoms. They had to get me and my three sisters—Leila, Rose, and Samira—and my brother Albert, to the airport, quickly.

"Hurry! It's not far, but we need to hurry," my mother told us.

"Why?" I asked.

"What's the rush?" my older sister Leila, who was fifteen, asked.

"No more questions. Get dressed and in that car, now!"

My mother and the five of us crammed ourselves into the back seat. My father sat in the front, next to his good friend Farouk Abu Aljuban, who had offered to drive us to the airport. With friends in different Palestinian circles, Farouk could help us pass through roadblocks and checkpoints.

As we drove off I looked back, out the car's rear window, and glimpsed our home. Then everything faded away, except for the sounds of gunshots all the way to the airport.

At the airport, my father showed a security officer our British passports, identifying us as Palestinians, since Palestine was under British Mandate rule. He ushered us into a small plane. As we took off, my mother turned to my father and asked if he'd made sure the house was safely locked.

"Yes. Why?"

"I don't want to return and find that someone has broken into our home and stolen everything," she explained.

The plane carried fourteen passengers, seven from my family. The short flight from Jaffa to Beirut airport hurried us away—from our home and our familiar identities. On the morning of April 14, 1948, we became a family of refugees, and together as a family we fled to many places, but never back to Jaffa. At the time, we couldn't have known that we were being caught in a historic dispute, one that would try our souls, testing our survival and bonds to one another, and challenging us to decide what it means to belong to a family.

2

The Toubassys

My paternal grandfather, Khalil Abu al-Layl, was born in 1870 in the charming village of Rashaya al-Foukar, in southern Lebanon on the western slope of Mount Hermon. The eldest child of Michael and Farha Abu al-Layl, Khalil lived with his parents, his younger brother Samuel and his sister Teresa. Khalil's father Michael dedicated his life to his family, to the Greek Orthodox Church and to tilling the fertile fields of his village, which is celebrated for its pottery. Highly in demand for its quality and attractive design, the pottery found its way to places like Damascus, Beirut and Istanbul.

As a teenager, Khalil found himself caught in the aftermath of the 1860 Mount Lebanon civil strife. Fighting had started in 1843, with an uprising of Christian Maronite peasants against their Druze overlords. The uprising culminated in widespread fighting and unprecedented assaults on towns and villages. Eventually, the war engulfed the wider region, including Beirut and Damascus. Old historic churches were burnt and destroyed. Christians suffered heavy losses in lives, status and treasure.

The civil war eventually reached Rashaya, with factions launching brutal assaults against one another. Many Christians in the region saw no future for themselves and fled in waves to places like Australia and the Americas.[1]

At sixteen, Khalil couldn't afford to join them. But following his daring nature, he looked for other places in the region to build a new life. One morning, he took off on the back of a donkey, with few provisions but many blessings from his parents.

His brother Samuel remained behind in the village monastery, training to become a monk. His sister Teresa stayed with her parents, waiting to enter a convent and become a nun. Her dream came true when she was admitted to one in Maa'lula, a town in Syria where Aramaic—the language of Jesus—is still spoken.

The first stop for Khalil was Ottoman Al-Salt, a town east of the Jordan River with a large Christian population. For several years, he lived and worked as a helper to the deacon of the local church. But his adventurousness and youthful eagerness pushed him to explore other towns. The local church always seemed to be his first destination.

A church in Tubas, a Palestinian village, offered him a deacon's job, a place to live and a chance to make friends among the parishioners, who admired his charisma and enjoyed his sense of humor. He became well known there and served on the local council, established by the *mutasarrif*, or governor, of the province to issue marriage, birth and baptismal certificates, and help in local village affairs. The name Tubas is mentioned in several places in the Hebrew Bible as the ancient Canaanite town of Thebez, named after a woman who led the village's revolt against the rule of an unjust king.

Khalil was pleased with the progress in his vocation. If it hadn't been for the news coming from Rashaya al-Foukar, that his sister Teresa would be entering a convent in Jaffa, he probably would have stayed in Tubas, where he was well-liked and appreciated for his work in his parish. Through friends, he found a position in a larger church in Jaffa so that he could be nearer to his sister. But his popularity in Tubas followed him to Jaffa. It was in the Jaffa parish that my grandfather Khalil Abu al-Layl became known as *Khalil Toubassy*—the deacon from Tubas.

The respect he earned and a familiarity he was beginning to feel at mass each Sunday led to a profound change in his life. At mass each week, Khalil saw a beautiful young woman, named Rose Shaya. Rose was in fact the daughter of one of the two priests Khalil was assisting as a deacon. Week after week, he noticed her and felt more attracted to her. It appeared she took a liking to him, too, which encouraged him to talk to her father after mass one Sunday.

The father asked for some time to talk with Rose and to the family. A week later, the priest delivered Khalil some good news. Rose, the family, and Father Shaya himself all blessed the union.

~

My paternal grandparents, Khalil and Rose, were married and had six sons and a daughter, all born in Jaffa. There they lived in the Al-Ajami neighborhood, a mixed Muslim, Christian and Jewish area, located a few minutes away from Jaffa's breathtaking beaches.

But sadly, my grandfather died at the early age of forty-one, from malaria.

My grandmother Rose continued to live with her children in the family home in Al-Ajami district from 1905 until her death in early 1946. The house remained in the family until 1948.

When Khalil passed away, the eldest son, Michael, suddenly found himself the head of the family. He looked for ways to help provide for his mother, brothers, sister and himself. When Uncle Michael finished high school, he apprenticed as a dental technician in a clinic in Jaffa.

After World War I ended in 1918, Damascus University reopened, and Michael traveled to Damascus to visit the dental school. Established in 1903 as part of the Faculty of Medical Sciences, the school was well-respected in the region. Michael was pleased with what he saw there, especially when he learned that tuition was free for Arab students, an expression of solidarity. He returned to Jaffa, convinced his mother to let him go, then applied and was admitted. With his modest savings to pay for his living expenses, he completed the program and headed back to Jaffa to start his career in dentistry.

A few years later, he married Evelyn Sarrouf. Together they had three boys, Alfred, Emile and Nadim, and two daughters, Aida Mitri and Nadia. In 1948, they too would leave Jaffa, among the last to join the exodus of refugees heading to Jordan. The three boys would follow their father into the medical field, Alfred also as a dentist, Emile as a pharmacologist and Nadim as a medical doctor. The two daughters, Aida and Nadia Amare', live in Amman, Jordan.

Next after Michael, my father Issa was born in 1899, the second child of the seven. Unlike his older brother, he never liked, or finished, school. Instead, he always wanted to learn a skilled trade and start a business of his own. The opportunity came from our family's Jewish neighbors, when Rachel, a good friend of my grandmother Rose, offered to help him apprentice with her husband Jacob, who upholstered the seats of horse-drawn carriages. About fifteen years old at the time, my father took the job and started to learn upholstering from a real master of the trade.

With fondness and gratitude, my father always remembered how skilled Jacob was and how well he trained him. He often recalled Jacob's saying: "Some people are gifted at working with their hands, and with a good innovative mind and passion they can become masters of their trade." There couldn't be a better description of my father himself.

During this time period of World War I, the Ottomans were losing ground in the war. Their army was depleted and badly in need of new recruits. Turkish officers roamed through the towns and villages of Palestine and Greater Syria, hunting for able-bodied young men to conscript into the army. One evening my father was walking home from work, tired, hungry and looking forward to his mother's cooking, when out of nowhere a Turkish officer grabbed him by the arm.

"What's your name?" he demanded.

"Issa."

"There's a war on, and we need strong young men like you to defend the Caliphate.»

"But I'm not at war with anyone."

"You are now. The train is leaving soon, and you're going to be on it."

Heading to the train station, the officer pulled him aside toward a group of recruits who had been assembled from the Al-Ajami neighborhood.

"I need to let my mother know," my father told the officer.
"We'll let her know."

The next thing he knew, my father was being shoved onto the train, already packed with conscripted recruits from Jaffa. Frightened and wanting to go back to his mother and family, he found himself heading for Damascus.

Miles later, another Turkish officer appeared, this one holding a clipboard. He sat down beside Issa.

"What's your name, age and religion?"

"Issa Toubassy. I'm fifteen, Palestinian Christian."

"A Christian! You can't serve in our army. What makes you think you can? Get off at the next stop. Go back to Jaffa."

"But how do I get back?"

"Walk. No more free rides."

It took my father several days to walk back home, where he was greeted by his by now panicked mother. She hugged him and kept repeating, "You're alive, you're still alive!"

After my father came Farha, the only girl among the seven Toubassy children. She grew up in Jaffa and attended the Saint Joseph School run by nuns. Sadly, I have few memories of my Aunt Farha, except that she married Constantine Kudsi and lived in Jerusalem. I never recall seeing her, and little was mentioned of her as I was growing up. She and Constantine had two boys, George and Johnny, and one girl, Alexandra. She died at an early age before 1948, and after the diaspora we lost contact with those cousins until years later.

Uncle Hanna, born in 1902, lived in Jaffa for most of his life and married Antoinette Khabaz. Unlike the rest of his siblings, he initially chose not to follow the 1948 Palestinian mass exodus but to remain with his wife and three children in their home in Jaffa. But in 1956, all three boys left for the US seeking better chances to get an education. Tawfik and Wadieh both built careers in engineering, Elias in education as a mathematics professor. My uncle and aunt joined their children in the US in 1958.

My uncles George and Peter both finished the Freres School in Jaffa, a popular place from which the British recruited graduates for its administration. No surprise that both uncles got jobs after graduation with the Mandate Authority. George, the elder of the two, moved to Haifa and worked with the Haifa Port Authority where he met and married Violate Farsoun. They had two sons, a dentist and a pharmacologist, both of whom settled in Canada, and two daughters, one in Detroit and one in Lebanon.

Peter, the youngest of the paternal uncles, went to work for the British administration in Palestine. After he came to Lebanon in 1948, he worked for UNRWA, the United Nations Relief and Works Agency, in Beirut. The agency was dedicated to assisting Palestinian refugees and creating employment opportunities until they could return to their homes. He later moved with his family to Congo-Kinshasa where he served as UN permanent representative. Peter retired in Paris, remaining there until he passed away in 2008.

Finally, a favorite uncle of ours, Uncle Mitri, was the second youngest of the brothers, born in 1912. He excelled in his studies in Jaffa, and this helped him earn a scholarship from the British Council to attend college in London. After graduating, he returned to Jaffa where he lived and worked until he secured a senior position in the British Mandate administration, headquartered in a wing of the King David Hotel in Jerusalem.

The British Mandate administration for Palestine had been formalized in 1923, with the approval of the League of Nations, and it continued until 1948. Well-educated local recruits were tempted with offers to join the service. Mitri was offered a job with a good salary and benefits, and with the added prestige of working in government. But he would have to move away from home and be separated from his family. A few weeks before his departure, his mother—my grandmother Rose—helped him pack. Good at needlework, she sewed his initials onto his underwear, pajamas and socks. My grandmother was of medium height, slim, with beautiful green eyes and silver hair. With her light complexion and smooth skin, she never wore any makeup. To this day, I distinctly remember her, seated in her chair by the window in the sitting room on the ground floor of her home, watching passersby as she did her needlework.

I was only seven, but I remember how much fun it was to be around Uncle Mitri. He used to take my sisters, brother and me out to buy Cadbury chocolates. And his move to Jerusalem never stopped him from coming back on the weekends and for holidays. Jerusalem was only an hour's drive from Jaffa, but to me it felt as if Uncle Mitri had gone to the other end of the world. He settled into his new apartment in Jerusalem and new job. But on the weekends when he returned, he took us out for our Cadbury treats, just as always.

~

The conflict among Palestinian Arabs, Jewish settlers, and the British Mandate authority had begun to take many forms—Jewish attacks on British and Palestinian targets, Palestinian attacks on Jewish ones, and British attempts to keep law and order. One trigger of the escalating tensions was the 1929 Passfield White Paper, written by colonial secretary Sydney Webb. Challenging exclusivist labor policies and the eviction of Palestinian tenant farmers from lands, it restricted Jewish immigration levels.

Then in 1936, the "Arab Revolt" began, as six prominent Palestinian leaders set aside their rivalries and joined forces, led by Haj Amin al Hussiani, to challenge the displacement of Palestinians. Responses to the uprising grew rapidly hardline. In an effort to quell it, the British allowed the arming of the Haganah, a paramilitary group, with which British security would cooperate until the revolt ended in 1939. This wave of violence broke on many families, and did not spare our own.

On July 22, 1946, unsettling news came out of Jerusalem about an attack at the King David Hotel. The hotel housed the British secretariat general of the colonial government of Palestine, and the military and administrative headquarters where our uncle Mitri worked.

That day I was with my mother, sisters and brother at the beach, not far from where my grandmother lived. I remember an uneasy feeling of expectancy in the air. My mother overheard people talking about a bad explosion in Jerusalem at the King David Hotel. Our uncle Peter arrived and urged my mother to gather up all of us and return home right away.

News of the attack was confirmed. But the whereabouts of Uncle Mitri was unknown. At home, my father and his brothers met and tried to find out more. Finally, they learned that the site of the explosion was the wing that housed Mitri's office in the British administration.

My parents and uncles became more apprehensive and frightened, especially when the radio news reported details about the extent of the destruction. Over ninety people had been killed, and many more were still unaccounted for, buried beneath the rubble. The severity of the explosion had made it difficult to identify mangled bodies, and the radio appealed to parents and relatives to join in the search for, and help to identify, loved ones.

Early the next day, my father and uncles left for Jerusalem to take part in the search. Along with other families, they combed through the rubble.

Finally, my father heard his brother Hanna call out, "I found him!"

Sad and dejected, they headed home. My mother met my father at the door and listened to him describe how he and his brothers had identified Mitri's body. They had spotted the initials, *MKT*, which Mother had sewn onto the pair of socks still on his shoeless feet.

In the days that followed the bombing, rumors spread about who had committed this attack. A main suspect was Irgun Zvai Leumi, a paramilitary group founded in 1931 that later admitted responsibility for it.

Like the attack on the King David Hotel, attacks on British military camps, banks and post offices pressured the Mandate

Authority to lift the quota of Jews permitted to immigrate to Palestine and turn a blind eye to immigrants brought in illegally by the Jewish Agency to Palestine. They destabilized British rule, showing how incapable the British were of maintaining law and order, planting seeds of distrust and suspicion.

Over time, attacks would begin to target Palestinian villages, many of which would be entirely destroyed or left uninhabitable, creating an environment of confusion and panic. Palestinian families would be forced to flee their homes, seeking refuge in neighboring countries. Lacking the tools to manage the influx of European settlers who were seeking to uproot and displace them, the towns and villages of Palestinians would be depopulated, then repopulated by immigrants and renamed.

In 1936, a nationalist revolt erupted against the British administration, demanding Palestinian independence and a reversal of the promise to create an exclusivist Jewish national home in Palestine. Finally, on May 16, 1936, Palestinian leaders called for a general strike. The revolt lasted three years, until 1939 when it was suppressed by the British, and Palestinian leaders of the revolt fled into exile.[2]

After the King David Hotel bombing, Mitri's body was brought home to Jaffa for funeral, and burial. From then on, when we were young, my parents seldom again spoke about Uncle Mitri in our presence.

3
THE ZAKKAS

My maternal great-grandfather Nicola Zakka was from I'billin, a small Christian village in Al Jaleel region, a mountainous area straddling present-day northern Israel and southern Lebanon. I'billin is known for its long history, to this day, of peaceful resistance to the Israeli occupation. At a young age, Nicola Zakka married Olga Saikaley, from a prominent Haifa Christian family. He was ordained a Greek Orthodox priest and appointed priest of I'billin. This assignment ended a few years later when the archbishop decided to move him to a larger parish in Acre. This port city in Haifa Bay became home for him, his wife and children—eventually six boys and five girls. Elia, my maternal grandfather, was born there in 1878, the fourth of the six boys.

Elia was raised by parents who revered education. Nicola and Olga had a great love for the Arabic language and its literature. When the Church again moved my great-grandfather and the family to Haifa, Elia attended the Greek Orthodox and Russian schools. He graduated from the Russian Seminary in Nazareth, a school with a sterling reputation. The seminary was attended by widely known authors such as Mikha'il Na'ima, the accomplished writer and philosopher, a colleague and friend of Gibran Khalil Gibran, the Lebanese writer, poet and artist, whose book *The Prophet* made him a popular poet of global stature.

After graduating, Elia taught at the Russian Seminary for a year. On frequent trips to Beirut to see his friends from Haifa who were attending the American University of Beirut (AUB), he was so impressed by the University that he decided to apply for admission. Fortunately, he was accepted and moved to Beirut.

After two years at AUB, he received a tempting offer to work as a correspondent for *Al-Ahram*, a prestigious Egyptian newspaper. He thought this opportunity in the writing field might come just once in a lifetime and didn't want to squander it. So he quit AUB and joined *Al-Ahram*.

For his first assignment, he covered the 1898 Holy Land visit of the King of Prussia and Emperor of Germany Wilhelm II, Frederick William Victor Albert and his wife the Empress. Thus began my grandfather Elia's career in journalism, a field he loved and worked in until the end of his life. The emperor's visit—to Damascus, Beirut, Jerusalem, and Cairo—had political and historic significance in cementing relations between the Prussian and Ottoman Empires, and personally between Emperor Wilhelm II and Sultan Abdul Hamid II. Abdul Hamid planned lavish receptions for his friend in all the major cities on his program's visit. My grandfather toured Greater Syria and Jerusalem with this delegation.

The Palestine question was ever-present in the politics of the era. The Zionist movement had dispatched Theodor Herzl to Jerusalem to lobby for a Jewish nation-state. It was no secret that Sultan Abdul Hamid II was no friend of the Zionist project. In this respect, he differed from other Arab leaders who, while offering lip-service opposition, were not unwilling to put their own narrow interests ahead of the struggle for Palestinian national and human rights.

~

In Egypt, writers, intellectuals and journalists enjoyed a measure of freedom of the press and speech under the rule of the Khedives. This dynasty was established by Mohammad Ali Pasha, an Albanian Ottoman commander who declared himself, with the consent of the Ottoman authorities, a *wali*, or governor, of Egypt and Sudan. His progressive dynasty ruled from the nineteenth century to the mid-twentieth.

In 1902, Ibrahim Pasha Zakka, my maternal great-uncle, founded the newspaper *Al-Nafir al-Uthmani* (*The Bugle of*

Uthmani), which he published in Alexandria. In 1906, my grandfather joined him as a partner. In 1908, following the return of oppressive Ottoman rule to Egypt, Ibrahim Zakka decided to transfer ownership of the newspaper to his brother, my grandfather Elia, who wanted to move back to Palestine.

Elia Zakka's story of marriage and family began on one of his visits to Lebanon for business—and fun. A friend insisted that he should meet a young woman from Tripoli, Julia Tueni, the daughter of a respected grain trader, Anton Tueni. The Tuenis were more than grain traders. To this day, they are involved in politics and journalism. In 1933, the Beirut daily newspaper *An-Nahar* (*The Day*) honored the family for their sacrifices for freedom of speech and the press in Lebanon. Gibran Ghassan Tueni, Lebanese politician and former editor and publisher of the daily paper *An Nahar* (established by his grandfather in 1933), was among the new Lebanese generation who paid the ultimate price in the struggle for their country's independence. He was assassinated on December 12, 2005.

It was spring, the best season to visit Tripoli, a place, like Jaffa, famous for the scent of orange blossoms. They first met at the home of Julia's family, in the presence of her father. Elia liked this petite young lady and kept coming back to Tripoli to see her. On his fourth visit, he proposed. Her father accepted on behalf of his daughter.

The couple would be blessed with five sons and three daughters, including my mother, Marie, born in Haifa in 1911.

In Jerusalem, Elia published the newspaper *Al-Nafir al-Uthmani* on his own under the name of *Al-Nafir* (*The Bugle*). It was a political and current affairs newspaper, among the few regularly published in Palestine. Later, he published it for a short stint in Jaffa, and in 1913 Haifa became its home.[3] Like most newspapers, it suspended publication during the First World War. Publication resumed on September 23, 1919, with a name change for a brief time to *Al-Sa'iqa*, before the old name *Al-Nafir* was restored.

In 1921, Elia Zakka founded another newspaper called *Haifa*, which ran for several years, focusing on workers and labor issues.

In the early days of the Mandate, *Al-Nafir* posted official government announcements, as well as advertisements from Jewish businesses, raising concerns with some about its political direction. Others argued that on many occasions the paper took critical stances toward Mandate authorities, Zionist activities and Palestinian leadership identified with the hardline nationalist movements.

Elia Zakka was among those who early on recognized the threat posed by the exclusivism of the Zionist movement. Pragmatic and independent in spirit, he believed that coexistence was the only way to prevent future conflicts, an unpopular stand which made him a controversial figure within his own community.

In 1913, *The Bugle* published a weekly supplement in Hebrew called *Hashofar*, which was analogous to the Arabic *Al-Nafir*. In one editorial, while upholding "the banner of Palestinian identity," Elia wrote, "It rests with the two communities to respect the aspirations of each other and find ways to live in peace." This stance was not received well by Palestinians. Many critics denounced his call for coexistence. But those who criticized him may have wished they had listened. When the Zionist movement ultimately came out strongly in favor of a homeland exclusively for Jews in Palestine, Elia vehemently opposed the scheme and called on Palestinians to resist.

Elia Zakka died on December 1, 1928, at the age of fifty, after suffering from pneumonia. Dignitaries, community leaders and journalists took part in his funeral procession. My grandmother and her eldest son received letters of condolence from friends in Arab literary and political circles, among them Lebanese poets Khalil Mutran and Halim Damus; Lebanese writers Ibrahim Salem al-Najjar and Ibrahim Munzer; and Palestinian businessman Salem Abdul Rahman.

Anis Kashkosh, a well-known journalist, described the funeral procession in *Al-Nafir*.

> At 3:00 pm the procession started from the family home in Haifa on Jaffa Street, with male and female school students at the front of the procession…then scout troops carrying flags at half-staff, representatives of secular societies, a music band from the Salesian College, a Catholic band. They were followed by Christian Maronite pall bearers, wreath bearers, clergy from different religions, led by his Eminence the Greek Orthodox Archbishop and the hearse covered with flowers. Behind it was deceased's family, and then crowds from various classes, until it reached the Greek Orthodox Cathedral.
>
> Halfway to the burial grounds, friends and journalists carried the coffin, among them, Najib Nassar, the owner of *Al-Carmel* newspaper, literary scholar Wadeh al Bustani, who delivered a moving eulogy, and Jamil al Buhairi, owner of *al-Zuhur* newspaper, who spoke on behalf of Palestinian journalists. Another eulogy was delivered by journalist Tawfic Halaby.[4]

After Elia's death, his two sons Suhail and Zaki Zakka continued to publish *al-Nafir* in the same format, but as a bi-weekly. The eldest son took over as chief editor. He steered the newspaper in a new direction as a platform for ideas, inviting well-known and new journalists and literary artists to write for it. Writers such as Palestinian poet Abdul Ghani Alkarmi, Anis Kashkosh (a journalist who served briefly as an editor of *Al- Nafir*), and Lebanese-Palestinian poet and essayist May Ziadeh were among the many who contributed to its pages, until it ceased publication in 1945. And through the paper, my grandfather fostered my mother's desire to write.

My mother was in her late teens when her father died. All my life, she never failed to tell me how lucky and grateful she felt to have been raised in a family that provided her with opportunities. She and all of her five brothers and two sisters were fortunate to attend good schools, wear fine clothes and together enjoy the Zakka family's box in Haifa's big cinema, *Hadara Carmel,* as well as rides in the family's Ford Model T— as they were among the very few early owners of the vehicle in Palestine at the time.

Her father's respect for her ideas and his encouragement to write inspired her to publish several articles in *Al-Nafir,* reflecting on politics and expressing her anger with the British occupation. When he died, my mother lost not only a father, but a mentor.

4
LOVE IN HAIFA

My mother met my father through a family friend, Theodore Sarrouf, the owner of an advertising agency and a mutual friend of her brother Suhail and of my father. When they first met in 1930, my father was thirty-one and my mother, twenty.

According to their versions of the story, upon entering the Zakka family home in Haifa, my father stared at the tall, elegantly dressed woman and fell in love with her instantly. My mother looked at the man who stood no taller than she and wondered why Mr. Sarrouf had bothered to introduce her to this businessman from Jaffa. Theodore, the matchmaker of this arranged meeting, hoped that Marie might be willing to at least talk with Issa. My mother's mother and her brother Suhail were also present.

My father was quietly impressed by the family's old home, with its amazing view of the Haifa Bay. For her part, my mother had visited Jaffa many times with her late father, mostly when shopping in Tel Aviv.

He expressed his sympathies, and she spoke about the difficulties of coping with the family's loss. He quickly realized that she appeared to be keen to know more about him, about his family and his life and work in Jaffa.

My father told her about his early childhood in Al-Ajami district. He explained that he wasn't interested in school but had always wanted to work on his own. He was fortunate to have learned a skilled trade from a Jewish neighbor and now had his own business. He had started with upholstery for horse-drawn carriages, skills he later adapted to automobile upholstery when autos replaced horses and carriages on Jaffa's streets. Then he adapted his skills further to the new market, expanding to auto repair and painting. As the business grew, he hired several employees. His business could allow them to get married and support a family.

She considered his proposal.

On the plus side, she noticed his humility and was impressed with how he had built his business. She couldn't ignore that he actually was handsome, especially his sky-blue eyes. He had a sense of humor. To top it off, he was Greek Orthodox, like her, and he owned a good, stable business that would provide them a comfortable living.

But his limited education was a drawback. Unlike his brothers, my father had quit formal education before graduating from high school. But he did seem to possess business acumen—she was impressed with his story about how he had adapted to changing business circumstances. And with her father's passing, she didn't want to be in her brother's house, or under his control.

So, Marie accepted Issa's proposal and agreed to what would turn out to be a happy marriage.

On August 6, 1931, my father's mother and his siblings packed their bags and went to Haifa for the wedding. The celebration was one that was typical of a Palestinian Christian family in mourning, with plenty of food but limited entertainment. Out of respect to the memory of her father, the celebration was subdued. Yet, my mother was surrounded by her mother, sisters, all of her brothers, and many uncles and aunts, cousins and close friends. Several *Al-Nafir* journalists, like Abdul Ghani al-Karmi, who were also family friends, were there.

The bride and the groom spent the first two nights at a hotel in Hedara Karmal, a beautiful area for honeymooners. Afterward, they left for Jaffa. There they lived with my father's mother for a few months, until they found a home to rent and furnished it.

Having recently lost her father and being away from her family, Marie found it difficult to adjust to life in Jaffa. She missed the Haifa social life of immediate and extended family and friends. But most of all she missed her closeness to *Al-Nafir*, where she had hoped one day to fulfill her father's—and her own—dream of joining the editorial board. But by the time she gave birth to her first child, my sister Leila, in 1932, she had adapted to married life.

My mother gave birth to five children—Leila, Rose, Albert, myself and Samira. Leila, born in 1932, was smart in school and a hard worker. At a young age, she would hand over whatever little she earned to help Mother meet the household expenses. She married Alfred Farradj, and they had three children, a girl and two boys. She and her family would leave for the US in 1968. Our sister Rose was born next, in 1934. She married Camille Jaber, and they had two children. But during the 1975 civil war in Lebanon, they left Beirut for Paris, eventually settling in Luxembourg.

My brother Albert arrived next, in 1935. From his early years, he loved sports and was eager to go into business. So in 1956, he secured an immigration visa to the US. He was sponsored by, and lived with, a kind American family in Batavia, a small town in western New York state. This move didn't work out well. When he arrived in the US, he suffered a kidney attack, which required extended hospitalization. In less than a year, he became homesick and decided to return to Beirut. There he met and married Nada Kourani, and they have a daughter and a son. Albert built a successful career with a major insurance group.

Four years after Albert, I was born. Then Samira, the youngest in our family, arrived four years after me. After finishing high school in 1962, she took a job with a tourist agency in Beirut, where she met and married Gabriel Baroudi, an international executive. Samira and Gabriel had two sons. They would live in Amman, Athens, Paris, and Florida, settling finally in Virginia near their children.

While still in Jaffa, our family was growing and my father's business kept expanding. In 1939, the year I was born, he acquired the Jaffa sub-dealership for DuPont Deluxe car paint. According to my father, my arrival brought the family good luck. That good luck sign helped me hold a special place with him.

We attended church regularly as a family. My father was a heavy smoker and never gave up cigarettes until the last days of his life. Every day he read the newspaper *Palestine*. Big cities in Palestine each had their own newspaper, with limited national distribution. *Palestine* started in 1911 in Jaffa as a weekly, then evolved into an influential daily newspaper. The owners, his two friends Issa El-Issa and Yousef El-Issa, were Palestinian Christians. My father liked the paper's political line. It was a fierce, consistent critic of settlements that displaced Palestinians, which were viewed as a new form of colonial occupation that posed a threat to our people.

On January 28, 1930, the newspaper published a letter to the editor from Albert Einstein, who shared his conviction that the future of humanity should be built around the principle of a community of nations, rather than divisive, aggressive nationalism. Einstein encouraged the two sides to live together. He expressed his belief that the two great Semitic peoples, who had made major contributions to Western civilization, possessed a great future together. [5]

At the time, social life in Arab cities like Beirut, Damascus or Cairo was filled with many lively functions. Before the trouble erupted, social life in Jaffa was no different. My parents attended events for prominent historians, politicians, educators and other visitors from Arab literary circles and the arts world. Jaffa became a destination for such events, with visitors like the world-renowned Egyptian philosopher, author and poet Taha Hussein; Khalil Mutran and Ahmed Shawki, notable poets from Lebanon and Egypt; the "poet of Palestine," Ibrahim Tuqan; and Fadwa Tuqan, a prominent female Palestinian poet. These events were sponsored by religious-affiliated social clubs or secular societies that existed in most major cities in Palestine.

My mother managed the home in Jaffa and was a partner to my father in all family decisions. Unlike traditional Palestinian patriarchs, my father was a humble man. He wanted every member of our family to be treated equally. He never sat at the head of the table, except at the great feasts of Easter and Christmas. He always insisted that the food be served to us kids first and to him last.

At Easter, mother always baked special bread; I can still conjure its wonderful aroma and the taste of anise in my memories of those holidays. Not to forget the Easter cookies, date cookies were made with a hole in the middle to signify the crown of thorns. Nut cookies were shaped into triangles, to signify the spear that was thrust in Jesus's side on the cross. These pastries were a tradition kept by Palestinian Christian families for hundreds of years.

My mother was keen to keep our home spotlessly clean, especially the reception room, which held our family's best furniture and most attractive decorations. Reserved for visitors, it was a special place in our home, and it was always a treat for me to peek into the room. Mother would proudly unlock it when her ladies' group came to visit on the first Thursday of each month. She and her friends would gossip about news in the neighborhood. But as the security situation deteriorated, conversations switched to lengthy discussions about how to keep the neighborhood safe from militias. Many of the women worked as volunteers in social and welfare programs with the Red Cross/Crescent, on such projects as blood donation and preparation for natural disasters, and they later provided medical aid to Palestinian fighters. Some who were active in sports joined the YWCA to play tennis and other sports. Others became involved with the Christian Orthodox Club or the Roman Catholic Saint Anthony's Club.

My parents always spoke with regret about the Jewish Agency and its influence on Jewish immigration to Palestine.

In their efforts toward creating an exclusive Jewish identity, the Agency encouraged immigrants to remain separate within their own settlements and neighborhoods, even dominant over, "inferior" Palestinian Arabs, rather than integrating with those who had been here for years beyond memory. The Agency ran social welfare and education programs that strictly benefited Jewish immigrants, rather than also contributing their acquired European education and skills to their new homeland and its people.

~

Life in Jaffa had seasonal domestic rituals. Summer was cleaning time, a time when mother would hire Almunajed to come by to hand-fluff the mattresses. It took the elderly man all day—sometimes two—to restuff and fluff the wool inside the mattresses. Fluffing was a craft in itself. Using a tool that looked like a guitar, Almunajed would remove the wool stuffing, fluff it up, then shove it back inside the mattress covers. Mother would watch closely to be sure it was done to her satisfaction. After the mattress had been fluffed, sleeping in my bed felt heavenly comfortable. In Tripoli, when summer came, I missed the feeling of crawling into a freshly fluffed bed, and I miss that feeling to this day. Mattress fluffing as a trade has mostly disappeared in today's world, making way for memory foam.

Another treasured craft trade that is disappearing is the skill of polishing silver, brass and copper, traditionally done in the convenience of your backyard or staircase landing. Every year, Mother would schedule time with Al-Mubied to come and shine the family's wares. She loved displaying the beautifully polished pieces, shining like new, on tables and chests of drawers.

Another less skilled but important summer ritual was emptying the closets of worn coats, shoes, sweaters, shirts and the like. My job was to fill up the bags, most of which would be taken to our church to be distributed to people in need. Other bags were sold to a local door-to-door peddler. He would come up to our staircase, and Mother would bring him what was on offer, negotiating back and forth until she got a good price. She donated the money to charity. I loved listening to them haggling, a trademark practice of the Middle East. I'm sure this helped me sharpen my negotiating skills for adulthood.

Each year our church in Jaffa held its annual bazaar at the Greek Orthodox social club. Women parishioners would cook and prepare needlework to sell, with the proceeds going to aid agencies. What I remember most vividly from this bazaar was the *Karagöz Iwad* shadow puppet show for children. Karagöz Iwad originated in Turkish culture but had many offshoots, including the Egyptian shadow puppet tradition. A single puppeteer would narrate and sing a tale in Arabic, creating all the different voices and dialogue, while manipulating the mesmerizing shadow puppet projections of a parade of characters, including its main character—Karagöz, or "Black Eye"—visible through a white cloth screen. Luckily, our Jaffa puppeteer mostly stuck with comic tales, which made the darkened room burst with joyous laughter. But some tales were more serious, talking about good and bad, right and wrong, heroes and losers, leaving us wondering how our own stories might turn out.

~

But after shadow puppets, in the 1940s, going to the movies became the thing to do in Jaffa. The two big cinemas were the beautiful, art deco Al-Hambra and Al-Farouk. Both showed Egyptian films, with stars like Youssef Wahbi, Taheyya Kariokka, Sabah and Samia Gamal, and Western films featuring Charlie Chaplin, Abbott and Costello, Maurice Chevalier and the popular French actor Louis de Funès. The Egyptian star Taheyya Kariokka held a special place in the hearts of many fans.

Kariokka (1915–1999) was an Egyptian belly dancer and film actress. Despite growing up in poverty and domestic abuse, she persevered to become a dancer and created a school that made this art form popular and entertaining, first in the Arab world and later internationally. She became an icon. In the 1930s, an Egyptian Arab woman had the courage to revolutionize and popularize Middle Eastern dance, performing in front of mixed audiences of Muslims, Christians and Jews, from Jaffa to Cairo to Beirut to Damascus and other cities, in the same region that would later become home to al-Qaeda and ISIS.

My first trip to a movie theater was to Al-Farouk. As we walked into this huge, elaborately decorated hall with its attractive furniture, an usher met my family at the door to check our tickets and accompany us to our seats. After a long, anxious wait, the curtain opened, the lights went down and an announcer asked the audience to remain quiet, which did nothing to lower the noisy din, which went on until the film started. The main character was the famous Lebanese actress and singer Sabah.

Trips to Al-Hambra and Al-Farouk were not our first exposure to "the movies." But they were mind-boggling to people of all ages, entertainment at its best and a huge leap from *Sondoq al-Ajab*—the Wonder Box—a popular form of entertainment that preceded cinema. Up to that time, all we knew was Sondoq al-Ajab. This portable miracle was a wooden box with four or five circular peep holes, or windows, to look through and view a "silent film" of three-dimensional photos featuring exotic places from around the world and brief cartoons, while the *hakawati*, or storyteller, took his good sweet time narrating his elaborate presentation. The hakawati carried the box on his shoulders with a leather belt, roaming from one neighborhood to another. In Jaffa, his first stop was usually Faisal Street, and the kids from the neighborhood would run to this traveling miniature cinema, each of us clutching our five-mils coin with the hole in the center, to impatiently wait our turn.

~

Coffeehouses where friends congregated to play backgammon and smoke shisha were male gathering places. When I was seven years old, my father dragged me along with him on his Saturday—and sometimes Sunday—visits to the famous Abu Shakoush, a huge coffeehouse that drew many of his friends. His arrival brought excitement, since he was an excellent backgammon player with a great sense of humor. Abu Shakoush was a venue that welcomed both women and men, hosting famous singers, literary persons and authors from various parts of the Arab world. It served for several decades as an entertainment and social hub in Jaffa. The beloved Egyptian singer Oum Kalthoum, Egyptian-Syrian singer and composer Farid al-Atrash, and other artists were among those who performed there.

I always wondered why my father would bring me to sit and watch him play backgammon for hours. I suspected he wanted me to take it up, although I never liked or played the game. But the two long hours were always followed by a special treat. One time we stopped by a shoe shop. He got me a pair of Clarks, well-crafted with a new kind of rubber sole, which made me the envy of my siblings at home and of my friends at school.

~

As a child playing on our balcony and watching the world go by, I witnessed the early phases of the British withdrawal from Palestine. Long convoys of military vehicles carrying tanks and British soldiers passed down our street, a main thoroughfare, headed for the Jaffa seaport. The departure of British soldiers and vehicles was met with mixed emotions in our neighborhood. Some rejoiced that British rule was over and Palestinians were now a few steps closer to independence. Others feared a scheme for a divided state, or worse. The images of the British convoys, seen from the balcony, still seem fresh in my memory.

By the end of WWII, Britain was suffering from imperial fatigue. The empire was collapsing, and the British were abandoning their responsibilities as a Mandate power, leaving behind them nations in chaos and planting seeds of conflict.

5
STRANDED IN TRIPOLI

When my parents woke us up on April 20, 1948, I was a nine-year-old and didn't understand what was happening around me. My father and mother talked about the Jews and Palestinians, but none of it made any sense. At that time, they were counting on an intervention by newly independent Arab countries. Just freed from colonial occupation, they sent their armies to come rescue us, rescue the Palestinians. In reality, their armies were so feeble and ineffective that they were the ones that needed to be rescued.

Across Palestine, fighting had increased between Palestinians and Jewish militias. Safety and security had deteriorated. My brother Albert's boarding school in Jerusalem advised parents to temporarily remove students from the campus. My parents figured it would be safer for a woman to make the journey of thirty-two miles from Jaffa to Jerusalem, so my father hired a trusted driver to drive her to Jerusalem. They made the trip safely, got Albert and returned the same day. The fighting had begun to spread around Jerusalem, especially to the Sheikh Jarrah neighborhood of East Jerusalem, where the sounds of bullets and explosions were deafening.

At the same time, as fighting intensified in and around our Jaffa neighborhood, my parents decided to take us all to Lebanon to stay with our uncle Zaki for a couple of weeks, hoping the fighting would subside and we could return.

Our flight to Beirut didn't take long. Inside the terminal, we cleared customs, and my father looked for a taxi to take us to Tripoli. My mother's brother, Zaki Zakka, had lived there with his family for several years and owned a printing business.

Now here we were, seven of us, heading to my uncle's house to impose ourselves as uninvited guests.

~

We arrived at Uncle Zaki's home unexpectedly, without any notice, but were greeted warmly. They had an extra bedroom, which my parents used. The rest of us shared bedrooms with our cousins, which was fun. After an emotional meeting between my mother and her brother, they spent most of the night reminiscing and sharing family news. But slowly the excitement of being all together began to evaporate. It didn't take long for all of us to realize that feeding and taking care of two families under these circumstances would be difficult. Who would take a family of seven into their home for an indefinite stay? As a family, we felt that we had to move on.

My parents discussed moving to a nearby hotel. Uncle Zaki suggested the Plaza Hotel, and so my parents rented two rooms there. They hoped our return to Jaffa was just around the corner, but it was a corner we never reached.

Tripoli—Lebanon's second largest city—became our temporary home. About fifty miles north of Beirut, it is situated on the eastern shores of the Mediterranean Sea. When Lebanon secured its independence from the French in 1943, Tripoli started to gain a prominence akin to Beirut as a financial and commercial center. The Iraqi Petroleum Company diverted its pipeline from Haifa to Tripoli, then shipped Iraqi oil in tankers to the rest of the world. Many Palestinian staffers and their families moved from Haifa to Tripoli. In later years, conflicts with its Syrian neighbor cost Tripoli some of its trade relations and economic success.

Many Palestinian families came to Tripoli seeking refuge. Every day my father would meet other Palestinian refugees in a local coffeehouse, where they sipped coffee, played backgammon and exchanged whatever news they could get from back home. Some days my father returned to the hotel filled with hope; other days he came back downcast and gloomy. The days seemed to be passing too quickly. But time wasn't the only thing disappearing too fast—so was our money. My father had withdrawn some savings from his account at the Ottoman Bank in Jaffa, but not enough to pay for a long stay in two rooms at a hotel.

So, we moved into one room at the hotel. Some of us children slept sideways on the mattress, like sausages on display in a market. We thought it was fun because we thought it was temporary. As soon as things settled down in Jaffa, life would return to normal.

July came too soon, and our hopes for a quick return home were dashed. I sensed my parents' worry and concern. Over their Turkish coffee one morning, Mother said, "Issa, I'm hearing there's little hope of returning home before six months. What will we do?"

To make things worse, news from Palestine was becoming grimmer by the day. My mother's instincts told her that any return to Jaffa was off somewhere in the dim future, so the search for an apartment became a necessity.

Into August, Father came home day after day looking more and more dejected by the bad news. Important Palestinian cities were falling into the hands of Zionist militias. Jaffa had been a stronghold for Palestinians, but the militias finally occupied our city. People who stayed behind were being pushed out. As they did in other cities, towns and villages, the militias attacked the local population, which forced those who had remained to flee. Father heard stories of Palestinian homes being looted and destroyed. He heard stories about killings committed against Palestinian villagers, about whole villages being razed to the ground.

Unfortunately, Palestinians were ill-equipped and unprepared to defend themselves. They were left with no option but to flee, it became futile to stand in the face of well-armed and organized settlers, many of them Europeans with professional skills and education who had received military training.

As a nine-year-old, I didn't understand what it meant not to return. My brother Albert explained to me, "No return means you will never again be sleeping in your bed at home in

Jaffa." Later in life, I realized what this really meant. Palestine was being irrevocably changed.

~

In late August 1948, the Greek Orthodox Archbishop of Tripoli invited my father to his residence. He told my father that he was starting an initiative to raise funds from the local community to aid Palestinians who had taken refuge in Tripoli. He wanted my father to meet with schools and see how many tuition-free places they could accommodate for refugee children.

My father was elated to help. He came home with a smile and shared the good news with us all. My mother responded that she just knew God would never abandon us.

That same week, another piece of good news came our way. Two bedrooms had become available for rent in the home of a Lebanese family. The husband had recently emigrated to Venezuela, and his family spent time with him during the year. The apartment had five bedrooms, a spacious living area, two bathrooms and a large kitchen. We could share the common areas and one of the bathrooms. Mother thought it would be good for us for at least six months, a year at worst, until the black cloud at home had passed. So we moved in.

To ensure an orderly distribution of food and clothing to Palestinian refugees in Tripoli, the International Red Cross issued ration cards, and our family received one. This was a first step in officially recognizing us as *refugees*, an identity for those of us without one. At the beginning of each month, a family member had to stand in line to collect the ration. My brother Albert and I would accompany my father to help carry home our allotment, which included powdered milk, flour, margarine and, on occasion, a bundle of used clothing. The Palestinians who stood in line for rations included people from families of all social classes, from landlords to peasants, young and old. Need brought us all together in this line of humiliation, as equals.

To this day, I remember my mother going through the used clothing that we brought home. Mother loved nice clothes and wanted her family to dress with pride. As she rummaged through the bundle of castoffs, I watched her hold up one garment after another, wondering out loud about the boy or girl who might have worn them. When she held up a knitted red ski sweater, with a deer's head and leaves knitted into the wool, she said, "You can wear this, Samir." And I wore it, proudly, for several years, thankful to the American family who'd donated the sweater.

In an odd way, our life started to take on a normal rhythm. When the family that owned the house returned, we needed to find an apartment that had more space. In the meantime, Father had started working on the archbishop's mission, stopping first at the American Missionary of Tripoli Boys and Girls Schools. Mr. Abu Rustum, the director, was very understanding, glad to help during this difficult time, and offered to take up to ten pupils in the school year. After a few days, my father succeeded in placing some Palestinian children—including us—in those and other schools. My mother was thrilled with this news. She said to my father, "Last night I prayed to the Virgin Mary to ease your mission and to bless our family. She listened."

The first day of classes came, and as I walked to school with my father everything seemed unfamiliar. I was excited to be in the third grade, yet apprehensive. I suddenly started crying, telling my father that I didn't want to go to this school, that I wanted to go back to school in Jaffa. He consoled me. "Jaffa will always be our home, and we will go back. But we don't know when, so try to think of this city as *your Jaffa* for now."

The first few days at school passed slowly, but I made friends there. One day at recess, Ghassan Maroush and George Daher asked me to join them in their game, and from then on we played together. Ghassan's Syrian family had settled in Tripoli a long time ago. His father was a successful rug merchant. George's Lebanese father had an administrative job with the Iraq Petroleum Company in Tripoli.

"Where are you from?" Ghassan asked me out of nowhere, one morning at recess. "Jaffa," I said.

"Where's that?"

"Palestine," I told him.

"Oh. My parents always talk about the Palestinians and how they had to leave their homes. Did you have to leave your home?"

"Yes, and I couldn't bring any of my things with me."

"Don't worry I can share my stuff with you," he said.

I was happy to have a friend at school. But I still couldn't understand why this happening to me and my family? Why were we refugees?

One day when my spirits were low, my mother said, "Samir, you have to believe that God tries those he loves. Be patient and you will see good days ahead." Her comforting words helped me cope and learn always to look forward, not back.

Tripoli Girls School was coeducational until third grade. The teachers were very caring and tried their best to help me as a new student. When I finished third grade and moved into the fourth grade, this time it was the Tripoli Boys School, an all-boys school. It was much farther from home and it took me about half an hour to walk there. Money was tight—riding the bus was not an option. Although he didn't have to, Ghassan decided to walk with me every day. My used shoes fit poorly, and the long walk made my feet ache. Walking with my friend Ghassan helped ease my discomfort and raised my spirits. The walk was especially hard in winter, when the holes in my shoes meant my feet got cold and wet. One day it was pouring, and we both got drenched. At Ghassan's house he convinced me to go in with him until the rain stopped. When his mother saw us, she grabbed some towels and dried us off, made us tea, and gave us biscuits. She told me how her son always talked about me and how much he liked me, and that I was always welcome at their home. When the rain stopped I thanked her and headed for home. Ghassan's mom boosted my belief in the goodness and kindness of people.

The same was true about Mr. Tucker, our principal, an American. He and his wife traditionally hosted two pupils from each grade at their home for lunch. One time, I was lucky to be invited along with another fourth-grader. Our main meal was the all-American hamburger, with french fries. This meal was new to me, and I loved it! When the Tuckers realized my family's situation, they insisted I let them know if I needed any help. As I got older and met more Americans of that generation, I realized that Mr. and Mrs. Tucker—like many others—came to our part of the world selflessly, with a desire to educate and serve those less fortunate, and to build bridges of respect and understanding among people. Their example was not lost on me.

6
NEXT STOP, BEIRUT

It had been almost a year since we had arrived in Tripoli. One evening, my father came home dispirited after a get-together with friends. My mother was best at reading his mind and able to ease his worries. He complained to her that he was fed up and badly needed a steady job. We couldn't survive any longer on hope for a quick return. But like others caught up in this calamity, a speedy return was not entirely in our hands. "I should stop talking about my business in Jaffa," he admitted. "It's gone."

These were long days for my father, sitting idle with no work. Waiting all this time, he was eager to go back and reopen his business, but didn't know how or when we would be able to go back. There were so many unpaid bills that he didn't know what to do. Our family needed money to survive, and he had to do something.

Father had gotten into the habit of stopping by the Ford dealership in Tripoli, owned by my mother's cousin Zaki Attiyah, to pass the time. One morning, Father went there for a different reason—to ask Zaki for a job. When he returned home, he confided to my mother, "Marie, this was one of the worst days in my life. It was so embarrassing. I had to work up all my courage to ask him."

"And what happened?"

"He said *yes*."

"You should be pleased!"

"After all the years I spent building a successful business… and here I am working for others?"

"Issa, Zaki is family. He knows who you are. The job is temporary, just until we return home."

My father's suspicion, that the return of the Palestinian refugees was nowhere in sight, turned out to be right. Later, he would remind us that Palestinians were casualties of World War I and the defeat of Germany and the Ottoman Empire by the Allies. The devastation of Germany had set the stage for the rise of the Third Reich and the Holocaust. With the defeat of the Ottomans, who had ruled us, the British and French victors carved up our region into hinterlands they could control.

Palestinians mistakenly looked to the Arab countries as saviors. But just emerging from years of colonization, these countries were weak and had no armies to speak of. My father could see no reason to trust their ability to meet this challenge. He had no illusions about the situation, and was correct. By relying on the Arab countries, we quickly lost much of our land in 1948. In 1967, we lost what was left—the West Bank and Gaza Strip. The entire question of Palestine was lost—in the corridors of Arab governments, in ineffective UN organization and inaction by Palestinians.

Three grim years passed.

By 1951 it had become more and more apparent to my parents that our stay in Lebanon might become permanent. Tripoli was a relatively small city and offered limited opportunities to make a living. One morning at breakfast, my mother urged my father to seriously consider moving.

"Let's go to Beirut and see if there is more for us there."

"How can we move?" my father interrupted. "The children are in school, and I'm working at Zaki's."

"We need to find a place with better opportunities for the family. Let's go see about things in Beirut. How about next week? We have nothing to lose!"

With her usual persuasiveness, my mother won, and Father agreed.

Quickly, a trip was organized. Mother packed enough clothes for a brief stay, and they took the early morning bus to Beirut. Hotels were unaffordable and staying with family was common practice, so they decided on Father's cousin,

Hanna Shaya, who had recently moved there. Showing up unexpectedly at his small apartment, which he shared with his two sisters, we were warmly welcomed. Hanna had not seen his cousin Issa, and my mother, since they'd left Jaffa in April 1948. It was a chance opportunity to catch up.

~

Hanna's journey out of Jaffa had been precarious. He and his two sisters left on a boat. Jaffa seaport was crowded with thousands of people—families, children and the elderly, desperate to board one of the boats.

Hanna's job with the seaport authority helped him manage to get them a place on the last boat to leave Jaffa. Their rough journey fortunately ended early one morning with the sunrise over Beirut seaport.

They had left Palestine, Hanna said, when the fighting escalated. As it worsened, food and medicine grew scarce. He described how militias broke into homes, taking everything of value—Persian rugs, appliances, furniture, anything that could be carried out. The militias exerted every pressure on the people who stayed behind to coerce them into leaving. In the chaos, high-ranking militia leaders competed to grab the nicest homes for themselves and their families.

"How could we be forced to leave our homes?" Hanna asked. "Were we just naïve, scared, poorly trained?"

Under the UN Mandate, the British had been entrusted to safeguard the local population. Instead, over the course of the Mandate period, they made conflicting promises to the Zionist movement and to Palestinians, then hastily relinquished their responsibilities with a shocking lack of respect and care for the people whose lives it affected.

My parents' trip, though short, convinced them that Beirut might offer work for my father and education for us children. By the time they returned to Tripoli, my father and mother were determined to move ahead.

While preparing to leave, we still hovered around the radio, listening to the British Cyprus-based Near East Broadcasting

Service. We clung to the hope that we would one day hear some positive news. But, "return or no return," Mother scolded, there were financial needs to be met and a family's future to think about. In a desperate effort to find a better chance to survive, Beirut became the second leg of our journey.

It would take my father time to find work, a place for us to live, and schools to attend. Luckily on their trip to Beirut, he had run into a friend from Jaffa, Khalil Murkus, who had just opened a small auto body and upholstery repair shop. Khalil needed help and wanted my father to join him, and so he reluctantly accepted.

"I accepted the offer, but I feel this is beneath me," my father told my mother when she asked him about it.

"This is no time to look back," she responded. "We are what we are now, and we need to make the best of what we have. Remember, we're all starting over—you, me, the children. Not just you."

Khalil generously had not only arranged a job for my father but also had helped us find an apartment. With a place for our family to live and my father's job, we were set to go.

In the late spring of 1952, when I was thirteen, moving day came. Father hired a driver and his white pickup to come early that morning. The night before, we had packed our modest belongings and were ready for another move. The pickup was stacked high with mattresses, furniture and boxes. We were a Palestinian version of the Okies headed for a better life, not in California but in Beirut.[6]

My brother Albert and I climbed onto the heap of belongings in the back of the little truck. My dad sat next to the driver. Mother and my three sisters, for one Lebanese pound each, rode the bus with their luggage. From my uncomfortable corner in the loaded pickup, I could feel the sea breeze and was reminded of the morning we fled Jaffa.

"Do you remember the morning we left Jaffa?" I asked my brother Albert.

"Yes, why?" he asked.

"I cried when we left Jaffa. This move seems easier, somehow."

Beirut, with all its diversity and charm, would become our next stop. But none of us could ever have guessed that it would become our permanent home for the foreseeable future. Beirut was a place I would grow to love and cherish. It gave me a chance to receive a good education, make lifelong friends and enjoy an exposure to great minds of the Arab world, all in a climate of freedom found nowhere else in the region.

This move happened at an auspicious time for our family, especially thanks to a farsighted mother who early on recognized the need to find a more promising place to settle.

Trying times for Palestinian families like ours didn't deter them from safeguarding their families' future, and education became the passport. This occurred on a wide scale, especially with young people who worked hard, finished their schooling and got jobs in harsh environments like Kuwait, Iraq and Saudi Arabia, not only to free themselves but to provide financial support to families left behind in refugee camps. Skilled and educated Palestinians, the Nakba generation, whether in business, education, or healthcare, built the foundation of what today are the Gulf States.

That white pickup that brought me to the grand old international city of Beirut, changed my life. I had no idea how important the move there would prove to be. While living there, I witnessed the city's transformation, as it became the gateway to the Arab world, replacing places such as Haifa and Jaffa. Arabs from all over the region would flock there, as tourists in the summer to enjoy the pleasant weather and beaches, or as businessmen year-round to conclude deals in this oasis, Lebanon.

But our excitement surrounding the move was tempered by fears and anxiety. Uprooted again, I wondered, *why does this keep happening to our family?* My sister Leila complained to my mother angrily, "I am tired of moving. By the time we get used to Tripoli, we are in Beirut. What's next? Why did we leave Jaffa in the first place?"

Hugging Leila and speaking as if to herself from a wounded heart, she recalled for us how Palestinians with very limited means—both men and women—had resisted the transfer of Jews to Palestine.

"Years ago, in the Haifa newspaper, your grandfather wrote about tolerance, until he recognized the malignant plan to create a Jewish state. Then from the pages of his newspaper, he rallied public opinion and encouraged people to organize against the settlement scheme." Mother added, "I lost my cousin Julia Naif Zakka, a nurse who volunteered to help the resistance in the Wadi Nisnas neighborhood, when a sniper bullet killed her. We left because fear clouded our judgment, Leila."

~

Our new three-bedroom apartment on the fourth floor gave us a perfect view of the Middle Eastern School and the headquarters of the Seventh-Day Adventists. I loved being close to their athletic facilities, which I used with kids from the neighborhood. On this verdant campus, Leila learned as a teenager how to ride her bike. We appreciated the Church's generosity in opening their doors to us and our neighbors.

We remained good neighbors, until the day that two young Adventist missionaries came to our apartment, rang the bell and talked to Mother for quite some time. I heard her ask them, "How are you different from other Christian sects?" In detail, they explained the principles of their faith. Two things puzzled her: the Sabbath and the vegetarian diet. Adventists emphasize a healthy diet and abstinence from meats considered "unclean," such as pork, and adherence to kosher laws. Mother asked if they were a Jewish sect. The missionaries said they were not. Mother wondered aloud, "So what do you want us to do?"

"We want you to become Christian worshippers."

"We already are Christians—from Palestine. Jesus was from Palestine, you know."

There the conversation ended.

Once again, Father started looking for schools. Through the grapevine, he heard about the Beirut Evangelical School. This school was started by the headmaster of the Orthodox School in Jaffa, who had joined the 1948 exodus to Lebanon. The school went from grade seven to twelve, so it was ideal for my brother Albert, but not exactly for me. Albert got into the proper grade. My problem was that, although I had only completed one semester of fifth grade at the Tripoli Boys School, the headmaster of this school convinced my father that I could start in the seventh grade.

I struggled mightily to understand the lessons, but my mediocre performance produced poor results, except in math. A caring teacher helped me after school and made math enjoyable. My parents soon realized that the advice they got was more beneficial to the school than to me. At the end of the school year, telling my parents it would help me catch up with kids my own age, the principal decided I should repeat the seventh grade, a significant blow to my self-confidence. He admitted, too late, that making me skip a grade had been a mistake.

The school was the most miserable place on earth. The old building was not equipped to hold its two hundred pupils, most of them Palestinian refugees. The tiny classrooms made us feel packed in like sardines. The toilets were always flooded. Early in the year, at school assembly, the headmaster encouraged the students to use the toilet at home before coming to school. Too many of the teachers were part timers, or had little or no previous teaching experience. Most embarrassing were the moments when I was called in front of all my classmates to report to the principal's office. My brother Albert would be called in, too. "You probably do not know this, but your tuition hasn't been paid. Tell your parents that it's way overdue and needs to be paid immediately."

Usually, because of financial difficulties, his calls were not returned. A second call from the principal's office would be followed by a threat: "You need to urge your parents to find the money or the two of you will be expelled."

My parents knew that our future hinged on getting an education, but they were finding it hard to provide. When listening to our complaints my father encouraged us to persevere and focus on our education. "I'll speak to the principal and take care of the money." Once again, he repeated a message we had often heard before.

"When you are forced out of your home, you can't take the citrus groves or precious belongings with you, or even your livelihood. But you can take your education. This school might not be ideal, but it is what we can afford. Study hard. Education is your ticket to a better way of life."

7
AMERICAN UNIVERSITY OF BEIRUT

Months passed and seasons changed, but little else did—except for one thing. Mother would frequently take the tramcar to visit her cousin in the Ras Beirut neighborhood. Ras Beirut was a lively, progressive district, home to people representing different backgrounds, social classes and religious faiths. On her tramcar ride, she would pass the main gate to the American University of Beirut, which was the major station on the line. Through the gate she could see College Hall, which reminded her of stories she had heard from her father about the two life-changing years he had spent there. Every time she passed the gate, Mother's eyes fixed on it, hoping that someday, one of her children would be able to attend the noted school.

She set about persuading my father to move to the Ras Beirut neighborhood, to be near AUB. Amazingly, Mother's dream came true when she found us an apartment on Sidani Street, not far from campus. This move gave me hope that, just maybe, my parents would find another school for me.

Fortunately, the move to our new place went without a hitch, and we all quickly settled in. From our new apartment I began exploring the neighborhood. I would walk different routes from home to school and back, gradually becoming familiar with the area. On one of these excursions, I stumbled across some kids playing football outside a school. I stood at the fence, watching them. From then on, I made it a habit to stop by and watch them play.

After having spotted me watching them several times, a kid called out to me, "Do you want to play?" Did I ever, and luckily they liked me and the way I played. They said I could come back again and play on their team.

That day I excitedly told my parents about the kids I'd met, the school and how close it was to home. "What school are you talking about?" my mother asked me. The kids had told me it was called International College, a middle and secondary school, and that it was part of AUB.

The more I played soccer with the kids at IC, the more I liked them and the school. I loved the lush green fields and the students I met. I didn't just *want* to go to IC, I knew I *needed* to. One kid told me how good the school was and said I should apply.

Mother listened to my litany of descriptions of the school and encouraged me to go ahead and apply for admission. My dream was within reach. So I took her advice and, with my sister Leila's help, filled out the application. The following weeks were anxious ones. I waited impatiently and started to worry that I might not get in. Finally, good news arrived in a letter of acceptance to the seventh grade. With it, reality hit home. "How are we going to pay the tuition?" I asked my mother. "It's very expensive."

"We'll find a way," she reassured me. "We will meet with the school principal. He might be able to help."

So we made an appointment to meet with the principal, Lesley Levitt. Our appointment with him turned out much better than we hoped, or expected. His Lebanese secretary, God bless her, helped my mother explain our financial situation to him. After hearing our story, Levitt was moved and suggested we apply for assistance from the United Nations Relief and Works Agency, UNRWA. He promised to consider offering a small school grant to help meet the expenses.

"Samir," he said, "I'm pleased that you chose our school. I'm also sure we will be proud of you as our student."

The very next morning, my father and I were on our way to the UNRWA offices. There, a nice man helped us fill out the aid form and then asked us to check back with him in about a week. A week later, we were thrilled to learn that UNRWA had approved our request. Between UNRWA's support, and the school grant, my tuition and fees would be met for an entire year.

As a fourteen-year-old, applying and being accepted to IC, and then getting the funds to pay for school, gave me a boost of self-confidence and made me feel proud. It was thanks to my parents, especially my mother, who never took no for an answer, and an American school principal who extended a helping hand.

In Lebanon, I was a Palestinian refugee, deprived of citizenship and its entitlements. When IC issued me a handbook with my picture in it, that handbook became the closest thing I had to an official ID, and holding it in my hands was the first time I had an ID since we'd left Jaffa. The refugee document issued by the UNRWA told the world not *who I was* but *who I was not*. And even though it was valid only on IC's 75-acre campus, it made me feel equal to my classmates.

From then on, each school day I would wake up at seven. Mother would prepare me breakfast of labneh cheese and za'atar—a mixture of crushed fresh thyme, sumac and other spices—mixed with olive oil, spread on a slice of pita. With it came a cup of Lipton tea. A five-minute walk would get me to IC in time for my eight o'clock class. Because we lived so nearby, I could walk home for lunch. At our house lunch was the main meal, and on the days my mother had lunch ready, I felt lucky and ate a full lunch. Otherwise, a cheese sandwich and lemonade would suffice.

At IC I studied science, math, Arabic, English, world history, US history, civics and geography. I really enjoyed reading a thick book entitled *Adventures in American Literature*. In that anthology, I first read poems by Robert Frost and loved the one called "The Road Not Taken."
...I shall be telling this with a sigh
Somewhere ages and ages hence:
Two roads diverged in a wood, and I—
I took the one less traveled by,
and that has made all the difference.

Math classes appealed to me, thanks to the caring teacher, Mr. Musallam, I had had at the Evangelical School, who made math seem like solving puzzles, and through which I discovered the discipline of science. Civics made a great impact on me. It taught me the practical aspects of rights and duties as a citizen.

After classes, the school offered extracurricular activities, a practice modeled by American schools. One day we would converge on the soccer field to practice, another day we would attend one or more of the clubs. I decided to join the Arabic Society to learn more about our language. A good choice, it opened my eyes to the richness of the writings of Arab poets, philosophers and scientists, seminal works that have left a lasting influence that continues to this day.

One day at recess, my friend Samir Zaki recruited me to work on the IC yearbook, *Torch*. This tradition, entrenched in high school and college culture in American education, seemed like something new worth exploring. The yearbook was entirely the students' responsibility, and Samir happened to be the editor that year. I became the business manager, whose job was to secure financial sponsors from local businesses, an experience that gave me valuable insights into the workings of business. Samir would become a medical doctor at Cambridge University, doing lifelong research on the functions of the brain.

But the most long-lasting impact of IC on my life were the friendships with students from near and far. Among our close group of friends—our "Gang of Five"—was Walid Barakat. He came from a Syrian family and lost his mother when he was still a child. Her absence left him with a wound that never healed, right up to the last days of his life. A brilliant student, the smartest in our class, he never cared about his looks and always had a shabby appearance. But he was the best read, had a great sense of humor and was much-liked by his peers. To the kids in the lower grades, Walid was the "Siberian bear." They taunted him about his weight and disheveled looks. Even at that young age, he was a devoted Arab nationalist following in the footsteps of his older brother, Mohamed Barakat, who was involved in the Lebanese politics and nonprofit organizations. One day in our eighth-grade history class, our teacher, Mr. Tracy Strong, listed ten dates on the blackboard, each with historical significance. He announced to the class, "Anyone who knows the significance of the dates will be exempt from the class and get an A." Walid stood up, explained the dates without hesitation, picked up his books and left, saying, "See you next year."

Fawwaz Tuqan, mischievous and funny, carried the Tuqan family DNA. The Tuqans were known as gifted writers and for their sense of humor, their talent for poking fun at themselves, as well as others. Fawwaz was always a master of practical jokes. No one in our group escaped his pranks. A good athlete, avid long-distance runner and college cheerleader, he used his talent to subvert the annual Arts & Science vs. Engineering soccer match into a carnival, a tradition that continued for years after our graduation. After attending AUB, he went to the US and earned a doctorate in Semitic languages from Yale.

Lutfi Shakhashir, at six-foot-three a giant by Middle East standards, came to Lebanon with his parents in 1948 as a refugee from Haifa. Lutfi was obsessed with aviation. He knew in great detail every plane that flew over the campus. His ultimate wish was to finish high school, join a flying school and work as a pilot. His height helped him become a good basketball player. A gym rat, after finishing his first year at AUB his athletic skills won him a scholarship to study engineering at the University of Oklahoma. His dream of becoming a pilot seemed to fade away.

Ma'an Husseini, the last of our Gang of Five, carried the worries and the anguish of the Occupation on his shoulders, as politics took up much of his life. This could be expected for a member of the Husseini family, whose history has long been intertwined with the politics of Palestine. Even now, he and other family members remain active in the political, social and philanthropic life of occupied East Jerusalem. Members of the family included Hajj Amin al-Husseini, the grand mufti of

Jerusalem and a leader of the Palestinian resistance, and the late Faisal al-Husseini, chief Palestinian negotiator to the peace talks with Israel and a leading Palestinian political figure.

~

In our home, evenings were a time for the family to huddle around the radio. The 1952 revolution in Egypt brought Nasser to power, and with it a new radio station broadcasting from Cairo. No one from my generation can ever forget the program Sawt al-Arab, *The Arab Voice*, Nasser's link to the Arab world. The anchor, Ahmad Saeed—a populist hero—rallied support for Arab unity, capturing the emotions and sentiments of both young and old.

To many in the Arab world, Gamal Abdel Nasser was a hero. It was only after the 1952 Egyptian revolution that Western-imposed boundaries and political divisions, which brought such harm to the region, began to face real pushback. Nasser was the first to contest these imposed divisions, declaring in 1958 the creation of the United Arab Republic, a union between Egypt and Syria.

Nasser's charisma and Syrian sentiment for Arab unity brought the two ancient countries together. In the Arab world, while many wanted the union to succeed, others were skeptical about it. Both countries sincerely rushed into the marriage. Unfortunately, the arrangement proved short-lived. After hundreds of years living under Ottoman rule, internal and external forces undermined this first endeavor to fulfill Arab dreams of a unifying identity and future. When Syria seceded from the union in 1961, after a military coup, Nasser and pan-Arab loyalist followers were left in frustration and despair.

Unfortunately, only years later did I, along with many others, realize that Ahmad Saeed's populist sentiments were stirring, but mostly empty, slogans that rarely produced the kind of reform to the political and economic systems that was so sorely needed. Promises of fundamental human rights for ordinary people were never delivered—not for Egyptians nor others in the Arab region.

With no end in sight to our family's financial challenges, not a single day passed without my parents discussing their difficulties and how to make ends meet. They decided that my sister Leila, the oldest, should leave the school for nuns, Saint Vincent de Paul, and get a job. She found a teaching job at a local all-girls school run by the Church. Most of the students came from our new neighborhood. Leila, being only 18, found it challenging to teach girls nearly her own age. So she registered with the YWCA to take a secretarial course. Like many young Palestinian men and women, my sisters were eager to earn money to help their families. She found a job as a secretary for an executive at Intra Bank, whose founders were a group of Palestinian bankers. Fortunately, the bank turned a blind eye to the government directive not to hire Palestinians.

Soon after, my sister Rose followed Leila, completing a secretarial course and landing a job with a tourist agency. This helped our family survive. It was the early 1950s, and women in Lebanon were already in the workforce, both in the private and public sectors. Some were even political representatives in parliament. It's important to remember that Lebanon, Syria, Iraq and Palestine, unlike the Persian Gulf states, were more tolerant, more receptive to the ways of life in progressive democratic societies. But I never stopped wondering, if my sisters had not been forced to live outside our homeland, would their true potential have taken a different course?

Our family's financial woes weighed heavily on me. The absence of productive activities for high school students made summer a boring time and did little to relieve our plight. Lebanese business culture didn't permit part-time summer jobs for high school and college students. So, when my uncle Peter asked me if I would like a summer job, I was elated. The job was in a laboratory where I washed and sterilized syringes, then delivered them to hospitals and clinics all over Beirut. It was the first time I ever had pocket money to spend on what I pleased. I did the summer job for two years, with enthusiasm.

But in 1958, when I was nineteen, political tensions in Lebanon began to erupt, culminating in open armed conflict between Muslims and Christians. One cause of the instability was the presence of Palestinian refugees, who wanted to use Lebanon as a base to liberate their homeland. Sadly, Lebanon's history, before and after independence in 1943, has been embroiled in religious strife—in reality conflicts with complex roots where religion has been used for political ends.

Nasser's influence in Lebanon, as in the rest of the Arab world, added fuel to the simmering fire. Americans agonized about Nasser's attempts to topple governments friendly to the West, and Lebanese Christians worried. The president of Lebanon, Camille Chamoun, who was in the Western orbit, invited the Americans to come in and help restore the delicate Lebanese political balance.

I spent countless hours on the roof of the building where we lived, watching American planes launched from the Sixth Fleet aircraft carriers flying low over Ras Beirut and landing at Beirut International Airport. This presence prompted Lebanese leaders from all groups, under the patronage of the Americans, to sit down, talk, and end the conflict. Terms of reconciliation were summarized in the famous statement from Lebanese Prime Minister, Saeb Salam, "No winner, no loser."

In this charged atmosphere, after five years at International College, the administration chose to hold graduation ceremonies in a small indoor auditorium. Because of the security situation in the country, families were not invited to attend. This dampened the spirit of celebration felt by us, the graduating class, and by our families and friends.

8
BUSINESS AND POLITICS

In the fall of 1958, at nineteen, I was finally going to attend AUB. On my first day, while standing in the registration line, I learned that tuition of five hundred twenty-five Lebanese pounds was due—immediately. I stepped up to the registration officer and handed her my papers.

"How do you plan to pay? Are you on scholarship?" she asked.

"We don't have the funds. I'm a Palestinian student. What can I do?"

This woman, bless her, went out of her way to help me.

"Samir, I will go ahead and register you so that you can attend classes, and report that you will pay in installments. Meanwhile, you must apply right away to the Palestinian Aid Fund for assistance. I will help you get a job working in the library or the museum." This act of kindness, and AUB's policy that no student could be denied admission based on financial need, rescued me.

The history of AUB goes back more than a hundred fifty years. In 1866, a group of American missionaries—graduates of Yale, Princeton, Amherst and other schools—arrived in the Near East with a vision of establishing schools in Turkey, Syria, Egypt and Lebanon. Syrian Protestant College, in the Lebanese village of Shemlan, later moved to Beirut and eventually became the American University of Beirut. International College was founded in Turkey in 1891 and moved to Beirut in 1936, where it became AUB's preparatory school.

Admission to AUB was always highly competitive, but IC graduates were given an easier path to admission. A recommendation from the principal guaranteed a place in the first-year class without needing to pass a grilling entrance examination.

My academic record helped me get a recommendation for either the arts or science program. I opted for science, thinking that I would later enter the School of Engineering. It was my parents' dream to see me become an engineer. They had heard from friends and family about how easy it was for engineers to become successful and provide better lives for their families. Engineers were in high demand in the region, as oil-producing countries embarked on mega-construction projects. Little did my parents know how limited my capabilities and interests were in this field.

In early October, the school year began with a weeklong orientation program for new AUB students. I joined up with my friends, but also got a chance to meet students my age from many nations, and since as IC students we were familiar with the AUB grounds, we could help newcomers find their way around. A small group of American students attended on their junior year abroad to learn about the Middle East, its history and culture.

Some students from Jordan, Afghanistan, Ethiopia, Sudan, Iran and Cyprus attended AUB on scholarships provided by the US Agency for International Development. US policy makers hoped to win hearts and minds in an educational setting. Back then, as now, AUB set a high standard for diversity among colleges and universities. I remember observing my fellow students and wondering about them, their family stories and backgrounds.

Still, my own family's finances were a constant problem. In my sophomore and junior years, my father helped me a bit, but paying the tuition was always difficult. I lived with my parents and ate at home—it cost too much to eat out. Dating was common, but I couldn't afford the expense. I did get to socialize with girls from my class by hanging out in the campus cafe, which offered an affordable cup of coffee. In my junior year, I met Sara, an American from Boston who came to AUB on her junior year abroad. I enjoyed her company and admired her beauty, knowledge of the world and interest in Middle East history—plus she appreciated my sense of humor! But this relationship didn't last long because she had to return home after the first semester, so we lost contact.

My first year was a tough time for me when it came to courses like physics and calculus, both of which were pre-requisites for admission to the Engineering School. I had to earn good grades, and it didn't take me long to realize that I didn't have an aptitude for either calculus or physics. One evening, I was visiting my friend Fawwaz at his family's home. We were commiserating with each other about our bad grades in physics. Fawwaz' father, Ahmed Tuqan, overheard our conversation and advised us both, "Go see my good friend Professor Ali in the School of Engineering. Maybe he can help." We didn't wait to schedule an appointment with him. Rushing into his office the very next day, we confessed our difficulties in physics. Professor Ali got right to the point.

"What are your grades so far in physics?"

"Fifty-four," Fawwaz said.

"Fifty-one," I added.

Long pause.

"You two have as much chance of passing physics as a pair of mules. How do you expect me to help?"

We thanked him and left, realizing that our dream of entering the School of Engineering was turning into a nightmare.

It was time for me to reconsider my options. I thought about it and decided to go a different route—I requested a transfer from the science program to business. It was a decision I have never regretted. The business school had a fabulous faculty, a blend of people with multinational experience. As part of my studies, I wrote a report on economic development in the Arab world, under the direction of Professor Gunther, an American who chaired the department. When I finally passed my comprehensive examination, I felt prepared to graduate and find work.

As a student, I held several jobs on campus to pay my tuition—shelving books in the library stacks, working in the registrar's office, serving as a business manager for the new student orientation booklet, soliciting ads. For the entire time I was in school, I dreaded the future and couldn't imagine it. Would I have enough money for the next semester, for the semester after, and the semester after that? I needed to know that I could get my degree. Even when the road ahead was clear, I always felt fearful about tomorrow. This constant anxiety remained with me throughout my life, and despite my accomplishments it still does to this day. In those early years, the cup always seemed half empty, and the possible negative outcomes overshadowed the positive ones.

~

Student movements in the early 1960s occupied a front row in the global theater of politics. Students in the Middle East were faced with issues different than the ones facing our counterparts elsewhere. While in the United States protesters supported the civil rights movement, pushed for women's rights and opposed the Vietnam War, Arab students of my generation advocated liberation from colonial power and a just solution to the Palestinian question. Unfortunately, my generation and the one that followed after us saw our ideals defeated before our eyes.

Among my friends, the Palestinian-Israeli conflict was always at the crux of our conversations, agreements and disagreements. But we found unity when we joined marches to oppose the Balfour Declaration or to support the Algerian and Egyptian revolutions. Marches would wind their way through campus, out to Bliss Street and down to Parliament Square in the city center. Students from other schools, and from Palestinian refugee camps, would join in. Most ended peacefully, but at times Lebanese security would use fire hoses to disperse the protestors, mixing blue dye into the water to make it easy to identify protesters. But nothing dissuaded us from demonstrating, which was our way to be in solidarity with Arab causes.

During my years at AUB, Lebanese students expressed aspirations similar to students in other Arab countries. But as an independent liberal arts college, AUB created space for dialogue and for the chance to hear opposing opinions. Inspired by Arab nationalist sentiments, students rallied in support of the Palestinian people, against the creation of the state of Israel and the failure of Arab regimes to deal with the dangers and challenges that faced the region. Our life at AUB was intertwined with what was happening around us. Students represented many political movements and viewpoints. In a classroom in 1961, I would learn with Jews from Baghdad, Arabs from Mecca, Ethiopians from Addis Ababa, Sudanese from Khartoum and American students on their junior year abroad. The university provided—and still offers—a model for coexistence in the troubled Middle East, an amazing mosaic of diversity that has held together over many turbulent years.

For many of us, everything was about politics—morning, noon and night. The political situation in the Arab world energized us. If something was happening in Damascus, Cairo or Jerusalem—a military coup, collaborative agreement, an action taken by Arab leadership—we were eager to learn and talk about it

Students converged on the many cafes that sprang up in the fifties and sixties on Al-Hamra Street, the heart of diverse Ras Beirut. One mecca for our discussions was the Faisal Restaurant, an old establishment across the street from the main gate to AUB. The clientele were mostly professors and students from AUB, and intellectuals and political refugees from Syria, Iraq, Egypt and other Arab countries.

On one occasion there, a professor asked a waiter for a Scotch, but in a teacup so that students wouldn't know he was drinking. Then one day when the regular waiter wasn't around, the new waiter called out, "And one Scotch in a teacup for the professor," an order that created its own tempest in a tea cup. On a return trip to Beirut after the civil war, I discovered that the Faisal, where I had experienced such a lively exchange of ideas, had become a McDonald's.

From the late fifties until the 1975 civil war in Lebanon, most of the Arab and Lebanese intellectuals to be found in those cafes along Al-Hamra Street were activists who reflected the political mosaic prevailing at the time. This was a center where people gathered, debated and discussed ideas for bringing Arab countries together as we emerged from under the influence of colonial powers. Many believed our political leaders were corrupt and that only civil society was capable of making the desired changes. The presence of AUB, its faculty and Arab students, helped fuel this new phenomenon of open, candid debate and of speaking out against political leaders of the Arab world. Though differences and strong disagreements were voiced, they were peacefully managed over coffee and tea.

I still remember Beirut as a refuge for activists, writers and others from the region who were drawn to this great city. People thrived in an atmosphere of freedom not permitted in their home countries. Women could publicly socialize and actively participate in political discussions and actions. Many activists became political leaders, ministers, doctors, academics, architects, journalists and other professionals. AUB graduates served their countries well.

I was fortunate to be in the city in the 1960s and early 1970s. At that time, in addition to being an intellectual and financial center, Beirut had an international reputation as a destination for jetsetters and affluent tourists, something I observed as an outsider just after graduation. I still struggled to make ends meet, but on occasion, I had the opportunity to witness how the very affluent lived. An influx of foreign money in the 1950s and 1960s created the Lebanese brand of the sweet life on the Mediterranean. Five-star hotels sprang up on the waterfront; nightclubs such as Les Caves du Roi and fine restaurants opened to serve the celebrities and sophisticates who came to party in Beirut. Popular newer cafes were opened, such as Café Wimpy, the Horseshoe and Café de Paris. The Saint George

Hotel and Beach Club, a Beirut landmark built in the 1930s, played host to Brigitte Bardot, Peter O'Toole, Omar Sharif, Egypt's King Farouk, and others. Kim Philby, the British MI5 officer who spied for the Soviets, lived nearby and dropped by Saint George's each afternoon for cocktails.

Beirut's freedom was used and abused. It was abused by extremists and militants: International terror organizations such as Baader-Meinhof in Germany, the Japanese Red Army, Carlos the Jackal and others used Lebanon as a base to carry out their operations. That freedom allowed some Palestinian movements to promote armed struggle in refugee camps as a way to liberate our homeland. Military training camps were established and operations were launched against Israel from bases in the south of Lebanon, making the borders volatile. The Lebanese government saw this military activity as an infringement on Lebanon's sovereignty, which led to clashes between the Lebanese army and Palestinians in the camps. Palestinian presence in Lebanon continues to be a source of danger and concern that has worsened with the emergence of Shiite militias, and in recent years an influx of over 1.5 million refugees from war-torn Syria.

As a Palestinian, I watched in turmoil. Where did I stand? As someone who had grown to love Lebanon, I hated seeing it breaking apart. As a Palestinian refugee, I wondered if this military option might shed a ray of hope on our return. In the end, I became convinced that I couldn't influence the outcome of the futile conflict I observed, so I stayed on the sideline.

I'm proud that, since its beginnings, AUB has encouraged uncensored study and discussion of cultural and social ideas, many of which are still taboo subjects in some Arab countries. While there, I became eager to learn more about the state of Arab nations, especially what it would take for them to meet the challenges they faced. The school exposed me to a range of ideas offering different visions for the region. In this bastion of activism, students became engaged with the political movements of the day.

I especially found comfort in the writings and teachings of Constantine Zurayk. Born to a Greek Orthodox Christian family in Damascus, he studied at AUB and Princeton University, and became a persuasive voice of Arab nationalism. In 1952, he was named acting president of AUB. His views became essential to my thinking.

Zurayk coined the term *Nakba* (*catastrophe*) as the name for the expulsion of Palestinians in 1948. As acting president, he gave a series of chapel talks that had lasting influence for years to come. In his talks, he discussed the "spiritual aspects of nationalism," speaking out against colonial domination and arguing for freedom from such restraints in Arab nations. In his outspoken analysis, he attributed the cause of our Nakba to a movement that won not because of racial supremacy but because it was better organized and had won over effective champions in the British Mandate government, leaders who paved the way for European Jews to resettle in Palestine. Jews were better educated and looked to the future with hope to build a life for their own people. Palestinians were poorly organized and prepared, and always drew hope from a glorious past that wasn't helpful in this epic challenge.

Zurayk encouraged us to honestly examine the weaknesses and deficiencies in our own culture, in order to change it. His tolerance and respect helped me try to make sense of the violence and discouragement that surrounded us, and find a way forward.

The work, freedom-loving dedication and stories of many remarkable figures, like Constantine Zurayk, are woven into the history of the American University of Beirut, and they marked my young adulthood in lasting ways. The four years I spent there shaped me—socially, intellectually and politically. The adult I became is, in large measure, the result of values from my family that were strengthened at AUB, where I learned to listen to and respect views different from my own. AUB students were expected to contribute to the good of others, regardless of race, skin color or religion. At AUB, I felt at home and wished that my four years there would never end.

9
BEIRUT TO RIYADH, AND BACK

But my years at AUB did end, and after the festivity of graduation, hard realities dampened my idealism, joy of success
and sense of accomplishment. I started looking for a full-time
job. Like the rest of my classmates, I applied for ones with the
many employers who came to the AUB campus to recruit. I in-
terviewed with big corporations, like Procter & Gamble, Intra
Bank, American Life Insurance Group, Merrill Lynch. The
interviews all went well, I thought, until I started receiving one
rejection after another.

I was twenty-three. All this was happening in 1962, as
the region was witnessing an economic boom, driven by high
demand for oil and higher oil prices, which brought new
jobs and economic prosperity to Iraq and the Persian Gulf
states. Opportunities were opening up for skilled people and
bilingual college graduates, a good omen for people with my
background, but alas not for me as a Palestinian refugee.

I then realized the gravity of the challenge I was facing.
As a rule, Palestinian refugees were barred from working in
Lebanon. Authorities had to comply with the Arab League
Directives, which restricted Arab host countries from permit-
ting Palestinians to work or to be naturalized. The intentions of
this policy were well meant—to preserve Palestinian identity
and safeguard the right of return. But Lebanon's sectarian politics and sensitive balance of power among rival groups created
an opportunity for Palestinian Christians to be naturalized,
to help tip the balance in favor of Christians in Lebanon. Or,
depending on which group was in power, Sunni Muslim
Palestinians were granted citizenship. My father adamantly

refused to apply. He was Palestinian, he said, and unwilling to use any other identity. Every time my mother nudged him to apply, he was always ready with the same answer: "Why should I give up my identity? Isn't this what the Zionists want us to do? What if we return to our homes?" It wasn't until later in his life that he realized the full consequences of this choice. He regretted his decision when he saw how it impeded our ability to work and travel.

The unjust action of settlers, of the British Mandate authority and of Arab leaders, and the inaction of Palestinians, all put me in a quandary. What was I going to do? I was an undocumented Palestinian worker with a bachelor's degree in business. I hadn't worked hard to finish my education so that I could be unemployed. All I wanted was to help myself and my family, at least financially, to get out of the harsh life in the diaspora. I kept up my search to find a full-time job. In the meantime, I worked several temporary jobs that earned me a little pay, but no benefits.

~

Unbeknownst to me, opportunities were brewing in faraway places. In January of 1962, Saud Bin Abdul Aziz Al Saud, King of Saudi Arabia, had met with President John F. Kennedy in Palm Beach, Florida, where King Aziz stayed following surgery in the United States. During this and subsequent meetings in Washington, Kennedy and Aziz discussed how the United States could help Saudi Arabia introduce badly needed reforms in its public administration systems. The Ford Foundation, following Kennedy's recommendation, had signed an agreement with the Saudi Arabian government to help implement a government modernization program. Ford hired as many as forty consultants in the US, with various expertise and capabilities, to move with their families to Riyadh to start up this project. The Foundation's next task was to find assistants to the consultants, persons with college degrees who were fluent in Arabic and English. AUB graduates were ideal candidates.

In 1964, when I learned about the project through a relative, Elias Kourani, I grew interested. I got even more excited when he offered to actually help me with an introduction. The Ford Foundation project in Saudi Arabia seemed like a great opportunity. Elias introduced me to Haseeb Mroueh, a senior administrator with Ford in Beirut. A Shiite from South Lebanon, Mr. Mroueh had graduated from AUB about ten years before I did.

Very cordially, he informed me, "Samir, I reviewed your résumé. Your background and education make you a good fit for the job."

I was more than elated.

"The job will require you to move to Riyadh. What passport do you have?"

My heart fell. "A Palestinian travel document," I told him.

"Well, we'll see."

The Kingdom of Saudi Arabia was always concerned about security. As such, they weren't keen on issuing work permits to Palestinians. But Mroueh promised he would discuss this with his Saudi contacts and get back to me in a few days.

Here we go again, I thought as I left his office feeling depressed.

But after several gloomy days, I heard back from Haseeb.

"We got you the approval. Stop by the office tomorrow with your travel documents and passport photos. We need two weeks to process the visa. You should be all set to leave for Riyadh a week after that."

My luck had changed.

On the way to his office the next day, what had just happened kept turning over and over in my mind. *Zionists, Arabs and Lebanese conspire to keep me out of a job. Then the Ford Foundation says to me, "Here's a job for you. Let's get to work."* Afterward, on my way back home, it hit me. *I'm finally joining the time-honored tradition of having a job*! I even started to imagine having a monthly salary and benefits, and what life might be like with a paycheck appearing on your desk at the end of each month.

As cities go, Riyadh had a reputation of being dull, with its harsh weather and very conservative lifestyle. I didn't know much about the kingdom's history. In the few weeks prior to my departure, I read a few books to familiarize myself with the place and its inhabitants.

Riyadh had always occupied a significant place in the history of the royal family. By 1926, with the help of the British government, King Abdul Aziz expanded his rule to most of the Arabian Peninsula. In 1932, he named his kingdom Saudi Arabia, and Riyadh its capital.

Previously, Jeddah on the Red Sea was the country's de facto capital, a gateway port city for pilgrims traveling to Mecca and Medina, the kingdom's financial center, and the seat for governmental ministries and foreign embassies. Riyadh gained prominence when Abdul Aziz died in 1953. His son Saud became the king and helped transform the city from an isolated village into a spacious metropolis, affirming its position as the real capital. The city remained conservative, under the influence of religious groups and the teachings of Mohammad ibn Abd al-Wahhab, a pious preacher and scholar who wanted to return Islam to the simplicity of the days of the Prophet. A strict Wahhabi interpretation of Islam has long guided and influenced the kingdom.

As it turned out, the day in June 1964 that I was scheduled to fly to Riyadh on Saudi Airlines, I met Dr. Bloom, a senior economist with the Ford Foundation. He was on the same flight for a work visit. Upon arrival at the airport, a representative from the Saudi Institute of Public Administration met us, and we walked with him on a dirt road from the terminal to the Sahara Palace Hotel, a few minutes away.

The next morning at breakfast, Dr. Bloom told me about his appointment with the minister of education and asked me to join him. The driver took us first to Ford's offices and then to the Ministry. The minister was Prince Fahed bin Abdul Aziz, who would later become king of Saudi Arabia. As we entered his office, we were warmly greeted by the prince, a large man with a charming personality. A coffee boy entered and served us Saudi coffee, not regular coffee but boiled cardamom seeds.

"Sit next to the minister," Dr. Bloom told me. To my surprise, the prince didn't speak much English. During the meeting, Dr. Bloom made a short presentation about the Ford Foundation project. Then I did my best to interpret. What took Bloom a few minutes to say, I translated into Arabic in just a few seconds—not a good sign.

The minister noticed the hesitation on my face and finally turned to me and, in Arabic, asked me, "My son, are you sure you're providing the right translation?"

"Honestly, your highness," I replied, "this is my first day on the job. English is my second language. I promise I'll do better in the future."

"No need to worry, son. We all have to start somewhere," Prince Fahed responded.

I was one of the first Ford assistant consultants to arrive in Riyadh. Others began arriving soon after, including several of my friends from AUB. We shared a small house on the outskirts of the city equipped with desert coolers, a form of air conditioning generally used in high-temperature, arid environments. They provided us with a pleasant environment, a relief from the growling heat outside.

This was the first time in my life that I lived away from home, and it gave me a new sense of responsibility and a great feeling of independence. No doubt, the thing I missed most was my mother's cooking. But I was thrilled when I got my first monthly paycheck and was able to send back to my parents the better part of my salary to help them with our family's financial burdens. Most Palestinian families relied on this kind of support from family members for survival.

Within a few weeks, the number of assistant consultants increased to ten. I was assigned to the team of consultants in the Ministry of Finance. John Palsrok, a former senior staff member at the US Federal Office of Management and Budget, was our team leader. He expected me, as a bilingual, to build needed ties with the ministry's staff to help the team accomplish its mission, a role I enjoyed immensely and one that helped me build ongoing friendships.

His Royal Highness Prince Mossad bin Abdul Rahman, a senior member of the royal family and brother of King Abdul Aziz, the kingdom's founder, was the minister of finance. He championed modernization. Being a powerful figure in the country's political and economic life, he supported King Faisal's ambitious plans to reform the public administration systems. I got to work closely with him and others on his team.

Elvin Warner arrived with his family from Provo, Utah. Two other consultants arrived soon afterward with their families. All were Mormons from Brigham Young University. I had never heard about Mormonism before I met Elvin, who was a few years older than me and had never been outside the US. Unlike other Mormons, Elvin did not travel abroad as a young missionary. He became an elder Mormon through his missionary work in the States.

Palsrok introduced Elvin to the team. It was another chance for him to reiterate the scope of our assignment, creating a modern budgeting system adaptable to the needs of the Saudi government, and bring everyone from the ministry's senior management on board.

~

The high point of my assignment in Riyadh was a trip to Taif, the Saudi summer capital. The minister of finance asked our team to join him in presenting the budget to the king. The minister, a frail, old man, walked with a cane. As we were boarding the plane I offered my help, "Thank you and God bless you, son," he said. On the flight he wanted to know more about me.

I shared my story with him and told him how my parents fled in 1948 to Lebanon, about growing up in Beirut and attending the American University of Beirut. "The Palestinian Nakba is a dark day in Arab history," he said. "Don't lose hope. God willing, you will soon be returning to your home in Palestine."

Unfortunately, many Arab leaders showed similar innocence and naïveté in grasping the depth and seriousness of the creation of the state of Israel, not only for a million Palestinians but for the entire region.

On that trip to Taif, I realized how fortunate it was for a young man in his twenties like me—a jobless refugee—through a twist of luck to find access to the highest level of Saudi government officials and be able to learn the workings of the country's systems. The next day, we flew back to the daily work routine in Riyadh.

As it turned out, living in Riyadh was very tough and the weather was harsh. Temperatures ranging from one hundred ten to one hundred forty degrees Fahrenheit, coupled with sandstorms, made life in Riyadh miserable. Social life in the city was almost nonexistent. I was lucky to be invited to the homes of cosmopolitan Saudi friends who had attended IC and AUB, and they included me with their families on nighttime picnics in the desert.

One Friday morning in autumn 1966, an American colleague named Bill, from the Ford Foundation, came to our house. "I hear that after Friday prayers there will be a lashing of a man and the stoning of a woman," he informed us. "Are any of you interested in joining me to watch the spectacle?" Non-Muslims were prohibited at these events, and taking pictures was absolutely forbidden, but Bill insisted on going and encouraged us to come along. Hesitantly, I agreed, as did other colleagues.

Off we went in a pickup driven by a Saudi Foundation driver. Bill brought his camera concealed in a brown bag. We approached the square where hundreds of people had already gathered, and more were arriving from the mosque. The crowd formed a big circle, all waiting for the stoning to begin. A woman wrapped totally in black was led into the circle, and the Imam read the verdict. The woman was to be stoned to death for having sex outside of marriage. Piles of stones had been readied.

As people began hurling stones at the poor woman, I felt sick and turned away, unable to watch. Bill filmed the horror in its entirety. The woman fell to the ground, and a medical aide stepped in to attest to her death. He turned to the Imam and confirmed, "She is dead. Yes, she is dead." On this same Friday, another verdict was read. A thief's limb was to be cut off, for repeated theft.

This cruel punishment left me depressed for days, asking myself why I had attended.

~

At the end of December 1966, I left Riyadh for Beirut, where I spent Christmas at home with family and friends. One morning, a phone call came for me from the office of Dr. Dwight Monnier, the vice president of AUB, asking to have me call their office. Dr. Monnier wanted to meet with me.

I called and set up an appointment for the next morning. Administrative offices at AUB were housed in College Hall, a beautiful campus landmark. Dr. Monnier's assistant, Mr. Ajamian, showed me into the vice president's office.

Dr. Monnier welcomed me warmly, saying, "I've heard good things about you and the work you have been doing for the Ford Foundation in Saudi Arabia." He went on to describe a grant AUB had received from the Foundation to improve the planning and budgeting system. "Several Ford staffers told me you would be a good candidate to work on our project. Being an alum who already worked for the Foundation is a plus," he said.

Over the next few days, Dr. Monnier wanted me to meet some of the university deans and senior administrators. I met with history professor Joe Mallon, with the dean of the School of Arts and Sciences, Terry Prothro, and with the vice president for public relations, George Hakim, a former minister of foreign affairs in the Lebanese government. These meetings seemed to have gone well, and three days later a phone call came. It was Dr. Monnier. "Samir, we want to offer you the job and hope you'll accept."

"This is good news," I replied, gratefully.

"We'll need a couple of weeks to process a work permit for you from the Lebanese authorities."

I decided then to talk to my boss at the Ford Foundation and took a taxi out to the suburbs of Beirut, where I met with

Conrad Stuckey and John Palsrok. Both thought the AUB position would advance my career. They advised me to wrap things up in Riyadh before I resigned.

But when I returned to Beirut, I found that my appointment was met with resistance from the AUB's syndicate of nonacademic employees, for bringing an outsider into the administration. The union was motivated by two concerns: a desire to follow well-trod rules that determined who could move through the employment hierarchy, and suspicions of me as an outsider. Because the funding was from a grant to AUB from the Ford Foundation, and because the administration strongly supported me, tensions eased, and the issue was resolved.

~

I started my new job on June 1, 1967, in an office in College Hall that I shared with Michael Cummings, the assistant comptroller. One window in our office gave us a view of snow-capped mountains, and another a view of the Mediterranean Sea.

I was twenty-eight now. Four days after I started work at AUB, the Six-Day War began. A quick decisive Israeli victory left the region in turmoil. Lebanon was saved from any immediate repercussions.

I had taken the job at a time when both public and private sectors in the US were adopting zero-based budgeting. This method of planning provided a better way to control expenses, checking budget items more thoroughly, and required approval for the budget in its entirety. It was first adopted by the US Department of Defense. Later, with a generous grant from the Ford Foundation, the University of California became the first university to bring this system to higher education, an effort led by Loren Furtado, UC vice president for planning and budgeting. An advisor to AUB, Loren suggested that my colleague Michael Cummings and I travel to Berkeley to learn about this new budgeting technique. Loren and his team extended all manner of help to Michael and me. We spent time with the staff at the UC San Francisco Medical Center and with the budget officer from UC Berkeley. Loren invited us to dinner several times at his home, and he and I became lifelong friends.

So, we flew from Beirut, with a stopover in London. As the plane approached New York City, which I knew only from movies and television, I was overcome with excitement. This was real and not a dream. We took a cab from the airport to the Roosevelt Hotel in Manhattan, where the wide streets and tall buildings threw me off balance.

The next day, Michael made sure I got a good sampling of the great city. We visited the Statue of Liberty, Lincoln Center, the Empire State Building, and other landmarks. That evening, we sat in a Broadway theater and enjoyed the long-running hit, *Hello, Dolly!* One day later, we flew to San Francisco and from there helicoptered to Berkeley.

I had wonderful experiences on this trip, one of which was visiting my sister Leila, her husband Alfred Farradj, and their family. I was able to stay with them rather than at a hotel. She and her family had moved from Amman, where her husband had had a successful dealership for British Motors, to California after the 1967 Arab-Israeli Six-Day War. Neither saw a future for the children in Jordan after the 1967 war, and they decided to migrate.

And it was on this trip of firsts that, through family, I first met a young woman named Abla.

10

ABLA

Abla Hisheh's parents had fled the 1948 war for Al-Zerka in Jordan, where she was born in 1949. With her parents, she migrated from Jordan to Berkeley, California, in 1966. There Abla finished high school, attended Merritt Community College in Oakland for two years, and then in June 1970 was accepted to the University of California, Berkeley, as a junior.

She lived with her parents on Euclid Avenue in Berkeley, in a house with an amazing view of San Francisco and the Bay Bridge. Her parents and large immediate family, who number in the dozens, had migrated to the United States at different times after the 1948 Nakba. For Abla, Palestine and the plight of its people were never forgotten. Whether in church, at work or in school, Abla was always prepared to refute arguments about exclusive Zionist entitlement to the land of Palestine.

When she offered to drive me from my sister Leila's house to the UC campus, I was thrilled. This would give us a chance to get acquainted. Once together, we talked and talked as if we had known each other for years. Smart, sweet, attractive, a wonderful conversationalist—slowly I began to see who she was. Well-informed about politics, music or entertainment, she could discuss any topic, large or small. As a student she had volunteered on South Dakota senator George McGovern's presidential campaign, a learning opportunity on how democracy worked in a free nation.

Well-dressed, she looked amazing in the bright red Morris 1100 that her family had gifted her when she graduated from high school. On the radio in the Morris, we listened to Tom Jones singing, "I'll Never Fall in Love Again," the Rolling

Stones doing "Honky Tonk Women," and Neil Diamond belting out "Sweet Caroline." Driving in that red Morris, I fell in love with California—and Abla.

We went away to Tahoe for a weekend with five of her cousins, staying in a large cabin. One night we played the slot machines, and I won a big jackpot, $60, about $450 today. I hoped this was a good omen.

Finally, it was time for me to go back to Beirut. Abla and I said our goodbyes and promised to write each other. We exchanged friendly letters for over a year. Back at AUB, I worked, but thought of Abla.

As luck would have it, in 1970 I needed to go back to Berkeley again. One day when I was there, one of Abla's cousins was getting married. Abla picked up me, along with two of her cousins, and we attended the wedding. Afterward, Abla and I found ourselves alone in her car driving back. As we were crossing the Bay Bridge, I asked her to marry me. Looking at her hands on the steering wheel, I could see her knuckles tighten. My heart sank. After what seemed like eternity—maybe forty-five seconds—she turned to me and said, "Yes."

In September 1970, at the great St. Nicholas Orthodox Church in San Francisco, Abla and I were married, with both families present. After the reception, we headed for Abla's bright red Morris 1100. It was completely white. Her cousins hadn't spared a drop of shaving cream. I took the wheel and drove out of the parking spot, hitting two cars, one my brother-in-law's. I hoped that wasn't an omen, too.

We spent the night in Berkeley and then flew to London. In our London hotel room, on September 28, I turned the TV on and heard the sad news about the death of Gamal Abdel Nasser. It was a sad moment for Abla and me, and a tragedy for his supporters among the Arab nations and across the world. After a few days, we flew to Beirut, to find a city in mourning. The death of Nasser opened wounds from the 1958 civil war in which his supporters were a major faction. Everyone worried that this might lead to friction among the political parties in the country.

We stayed with my parents for a few weeks, while family and friends came to meet the bride. They enjoyed watching the wedding film. Abla got along well with everybody and began many new but lasting friendships.

Fortunately, we found a nice two-bedroom apartment not far from my parents and AUB. Abla adjusted to the new environment by enrolling at AUB to finish her studies in psychology. But Beirut wasn't easy for her. She often felt like a stranger. The people she knew were her father's uncle and two aunts. They provided a little respite but not much. Being used to California and its carefree attitude, she found she had to adjust and acclimate. We would be driving by the sea, and she would find a great view and want to go down and walk on the sand. This was not proper, as these free public beaches presumably were not for people like us, socially. Like most of our friends, our family had a membership at the sporting club, where we went to swim. Here, most of the beach was cement, not sand, like the sandy beach built on the rocky area overlooking Beirut's famous landmark, Al-Roucha (Pigeon Rocks). But Abla had the capacity within seconds to make you feel that—whoever you were or whatever the occasion—you were the best and that she was enjoying being with you. It was one of her many charms that endeared her to me so much.

I was the first of my close friends to get married. Soon our apartment became a sort of refuge for them and their girlfriends. Abla was just learning to cook, and having friends over for dinner was out of the question. So on most Sundays, they came over for a breakfast of pancakes and waffles—hence our new monikers, "Mr. Pancake" and "Mrs. Waffles." Our house was always open, and Abla made everyone welcome. I didn't realize at the time that these carefree days would turn out to be such priceless treasures, but luckily I was already sure that Abla was one.

~

In the fall of 1971, Abla and I would be thrilled to learn that she was pregnant with our first child. But a scary moment came when she fell down the long stairs of Fisk Hall at AUB, and went unaided until a passing friend saw her, picked her up and brought her to my office. I was shocked when she walked in crying, more for the baby than herself. Trying to conceal my concern from her, I picked up the phone and called the doctor, who urged us to come to his office. He assured us that she and the baby were fine.

In July 1972, our son Ramez was born. Both mother and baby were in good health. Two years later in October 1974, our second son, Ziad, was born.

Abla and me at our wedding, St. Nicholas Church in San Francisco,
September 1970

My mother's family, the Zakkas, around 1925. Left to right, front: my grandmother
Julia Twanie Zakka, George, Tawfic, Jaffar, and grandfather Elia Zakka.
Back: Zaki, my mother Marie, Yvonne, Abla, and Suhail.

My mother Marie Zakka.

Elia Zakka, my grandfather.

Annafire (Al-Nafir) Journal, issued in
Jerusalem, 1911.

My father's family, the Toubassys, around 1929. Left to right, front: Michael, my grandmother Rose Shaya, and my father Issa. Back: George, Hanna, and Mitri. Peter and Farha are not pictured.

Uncle Mitri Toubassy.

Samuel Abu al-Layl, my great-uncle.

My parents' wedding, August 6, 1931.

Mother's passport photo 1948, with Samira in her lap, and standing left to right: Leila, Rose, Albert, and me.

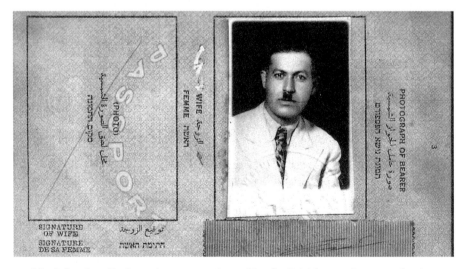

My father Issa Toubassy's passport, issued by the British mandatory authority, 1946.

II

11
From AUB to the Olayan Group

As I think back on my career, I realize that it is inseparable from my life story. Behind the goal-oriented achiever was a young man, deeply impacted by the Nakba, angry at himself and his people for allowing this disaster to happen.

My experiences with the Ford Foundation, with AUB and then with the Olayan Group, each in different ways left imprints on me and the person I became. These organizations gave me a temporary, but sorely needed, sense of belonging, which became my identity in the absence of a proper national one. They helped me provide financial support to my family. And they were the places where I regained my self-confidence. They also exposed me to environments where I could learn how to use my newly acquired skills, how to network and how to advocate for things I cared about within the business field.

~

I started work at AUB with confidence and belief in my ability to perform the job well, thanks to valuable lessons I learned from the team I had worked with at the Ford Foundation. This got me started on the right foot at AUB, in budgeting at the Office of the Comptroller.

My first boss there, Michael Cummings, was generous in introducing me to the university system. After two years in the position, management decided to separate the budget function from the comptroller's, creating an Office of Planning and Budget, and appointing me as director. Michael's instruction was invaluable in helping me to understand how the AUB system functioned. Sadly, time didn't allow me a longer period to benefit from his mentorship. A heavy smoker, in 1970 at age sixty-three he became sick and passed away due to complications from pneumonia. I was fortunate to have had him by my side, though briefly.

All of a sudden, at age twenty-nine, I found myself assuming the responsibility of overseeing the budgeting process of a university and teaching medical center with a 1968–69 budget of over twenty million US dollars. But I was convinced that I had the self-discipline, perseverance, ability to listen to others and motivation to work hard and to succeed.

As part of the planning process, I worked with AUB's president to produce the budget guidelines, set deadlines for budget submission and conduct individual meetings with deans and administrative department heads.

The process began with a request to the deans for budget submissions to our office by an announced deadline. This was followed by individual meetings. I developed good relations with Deans Prothro from Arts and Science, Ray Ghosn of Engineering and Architecture, Stanley Swenson from the School of Agriculture and Food Sciences, Craig Lichtenwarner from the Medical Faculties and AUB Medical Center, David Egee from AUB Medical Center, and John Gill, administrative and physical plant support, as well as with a number of administrative directors.

I found myself initiating and steering discussions, negotiating for more faculty and new programs, buildings and equipment, guided by the president's vision. I always enjoyed working with academics, because of their intellectual curiosity, integrity, and dedication to progress.

From when I first started working at AUB in 1967, to when I left nine years later in 1976, the annual budget nearly doubled to over forty million dollars.

I couldn't but wonder at times how a newcomer and Palestinian refugee like myself had been allowed and welcomed to work with such a distinguished group of people, who treated me with such genuine humility and respect. Their faith in me and support restored my confidence in the goodness of people, which my family's story had shaken.

For years, AUB relied on financial support from the US Government. Most of this was awarded as general support. The rest was provided as full scholarships for students, amounting to eight million dollars. Both funds came to the university through the US Agency for International Development and were approved by Congress as part of the US foreign aid appropriation assigned to American colleges and hospitals.

To our great disappointment, starting in 1974 our annual share was reduced by half. Political lobbying unfriendly to AUB pressured the US Congress to make the cuts. In an effort to appeal the decision, Bill Rice, head of AUB's New York Office, met with USAID in Washington. AUB comptroller Don Meyer and I met on several occasions with USAID officers at the US Embassy in Beirut. But our appeals were to no avail.

This major slash in our funding worsened an already brewing financial crisis that forced the trustees and the president to take a fresh look at university programs, funding and potential sources of income. The cuts in US support were key, but were one of multiple other factors, such as devaluation of the dollar and a freeze on tuition and fees. Our 1972–1975 estimates revealed a substantial increase in the school's deficit in the short run, one which could have a long-term impact on the funding of this unique institution that serves the region and has graduated many of its leaders.

In 1972, President Samuel Kirkwood, in consultation with the University senate and the deans, decided to form a Program Study Committee, with a mandate set by the trustees. The committee's task was to reconsider the university's vision and mission, with the goal of creating an economically and financially viable institution focused on serving regional needs. University Provost Dr. Samir Thabit was named as chairman. Among the faculty members on the committee were Professors Elie Salam, John Olmsted III and Nadim Khalaf from the School of Arts and Sciences; from the Medical Faculties were Professors George Fawwaz and Raja Khouri (whose son Fadlo Khouri is the current AUB president); Professors Raja Tannous and Nicholas Attallah from the School of Agriculture and Food Technology; Professors Raja Elia and Kanan Kano from the School of Engineering and Architecture, and I was honored to be appointed, the only nonacademic member of the committee.

As budget director, my role was to help the committee understand the possible consequences of their decisions, and how these could affect our deficit and budget. At that time at AUB, it was unusual for someone early in his career to be part of such a high-powered and accomplished group of academics. But a helpful lesson I learned from Dr. Fawwaz was to never stop searching for better solutions. On one occasion when I became impatient and frustrated with never-ending changes the committee kept making to the plan, Dr. Fawwaz turned to me and said, "Listen, son, there's nothing wrong with changing your mind. Scientists spend their entire lives in the laboratory, searching in trial and error and challenging the status quo. Without learning to accept change, people will never achieve progress." I took this lesson to heart and have remembered it ever since.

But at the same time, harsh measures needed to be taken, dropping programs and closing departments, all aimed at reducing the budget deficit. We succeeded in reducing the budget by eliminating programs we felt were nonessential to AUB's mission and vision. Several academic and nonacademic departments were forced to shut down, including the School of Pharmacy. But these cuts, coupled with an increase in fundraising, tuition and fees, helped us come closer to a balanced budget.

One gesture that touched the hearts of many of us involved in all this was when professors from the medical school volunteered to give up fifty percent of their salaries to help AUB keep going through this demanding time.

Finally, in March 1973, the committee's recommendations were submitted and approved by the board of trustees in New York. Upon his return to AUB, Dr. Kirkwood informed the University Senate, faculty, student council, administrative committee and the alumni board of the trustees' decision and asked for everyone's support.

It meant a lot to me to be part of this effort to help my alma mater find a way to navigate out of difficulty. I still feel grateful for the unreserved support I received as young staff member from Dr. Thabet and other members of the committee. Thirty years later, as luck would have it, Dr. Thabet and I crossed paths at an exhibition of his paintings in his native village in Deir al-Qamar. It was an emotional meeting with hugs and tears. Abla, my brother Albert and others who watched our reunion had tears in their eyes, too.

The measures taken by the Program Study Committee offered only short-term solutions to a chronic problem faced by many institutions of higher education, especially AUB. In America, private institutions most often rely on philanthropy, such as annual giving from alumni, corporate support and endowment, in addition to occasional hikes in tuition and fees. A tradition of financial giving is embedded in Western culture through tax codes that encourage and reward donors.

In the Middle East, this culture of giving didn't exist. It wasn't until recent years that people in the region began to recognize the importance of such contributions to fostering civil society. During this period of financial crisis at AUB, loyal supporters responded to our call, acting in a personal or corporate capacity. AUB is indebted to many generous donors, including Hassib Sabbagh and Rafik Hariri, among others.

In exploring ideas to keep the university financially afloat, I encouraged the administration to consider other approaches to funding. I proposed we turn our attention to our most important asset, the campus's highly prized land. The idea was to commercially develop a part of the lower campus land to provide AUB with a stream of income sufficient to meet its long-term financial needs. The board approved the concept and asked management to find a firm to develop a master plan. Dwight Monnier, my boss, asked me to lead the project. I contacted two firms in Beirut, American Express Development and Kidder Peabody. The candidate selection and approval process took almost one year. Dr. Kirkwood and the trustees chose and approved the offer from American Express.

Among the ideas we considered were granting long-term leases on some lots of land in the lower campus facing the sea. This would guarantee a steady stream of income to cover the deficit for the next twenty years, boost our endowment and fund expansion in the academic programs. At the expiration of the lease, ownership would revert to AUB. It could be an innovative way to solve our financial problems without permanently losing land that belonged to the university.

At the board of trustees meeting in June 1975, the American Express team and I made a presentation to the board. Among the trustees were prominent bankers, led by the board chairman Howard Page, chairman of Exxon at that time. They liked the plan and gave the green light to proceed with the next stage. I continued to take the lead on this project until I moved to the US in 1976. Unfortunately, the Lebanese civil war was taking a bad turn at the time, which forced the board to place the project on hold. The plan was later dropped altogether.

Another funding strategy we seriously considered was setting up a management company, where the staff and faculty could offer for-fee services, mainly to regional governments and private organizations. We hoped to model it after the Stanford Research Institute and the Ford Foundation. Emerging nations in the Gulf region could benefit from the skills and know-how abundantly available on campus to develop and modernize systems in agriculture, education, engineering, public policy and healthcare.

In the 1970s, healthcare was among the most pressing critical needs. The dean of the medical faculties, Craig Lichtenwarner, repeatedly received calls for help from Saudi Arabia, Bahrain, Iran, Dubai and United Arab Emirates. Assistance was needed in setting up new medical schools and curriculums, and managing healthcare facilities, such as teaching medical centers and hospitals.

~

During the post–World War II era, Middle East economies were witnessing fascinating changes. The oil boom had spawned all kinds of public and private projects, which demanded skilled engineers, doctors and business professionals. Putting these projects together required a set of skills and organizational experience relatively rare in the Middle East. The Olayan Group was one firm that had the wherewithal and ambition to fill the need.

This Saudi firm captured the attention and admiration of many, including myself, with their innovative approach to building joint ventures. They attracted key partners, such as Bechtel, the well-known engineering firm. With service offices in Beirut, Olayan was hiring for their businesses that were rapidly growing multifold across the Middle East. They had earned recognition and a reputation as a good employer that offered a robust working environment and that promised career opportunities. The strong economy at the time was helpful in creating job opportunities for many, especially Palestinian refugees, who were denied access to job markets, as in Lebanon. The Group offered college-educated Palestinians employment opportunities they couldn't find elsewhere.

As I learned from friends working for the Olayan Group, the refugee camps in Lebanon also provided a recruitment source for jobs in the harsh living conditions of Arab Gulf countries. Not many Arabs were willing to bear those conditions. For many young men, graduates of the UN Relief Works Agency's Siblin vocational training center, work in Saudi was better than no work at all. It was a worthwhile sacrifice in order to help themselves and their families survive.[7] Whether it was in insurance brokerage, consumer goods, construction equipment or the rest of the Olayan Group's business interests, the footprints of those unknown soldiers still remain for all to see.

Who was Suliman Saleh Olayan and what made him so unique? In his book, *The Story of Suliman Saleh Olayan*, Michael Fields tells a rags-to-riches tale of a Saudi, born in 1918 in the little town of Unayzah in central Saudi Arabia. Coming from a modest background in pre-oil Saudi Arabia, Suliman hungered for education. When he was still young, his brother

Hamad took him, on the back of a camel, first to the shores of the Persian Gulf and then on to Bahrain to finish his education in a British school. This was an unusual step for a Saudi youngster, whose education was usually limited to a mosque's madrasa. Suliman's ability to speak English and Arabic helped him land a job in Dhahran, Saudi Arabia, with an oil company, California Arabian Standard Oil.

Working as a storekeeper, Suliman impressed his American supervisors with his photographic memory—he memorized the serial numbers of thousands of spare parts and their exact locations on the shelves. He progressed in this job, yet his entrepreneurial instincts sensed better opportunities outside the corporate structure. With encouragement from his American bosses, he decided, in 1947, to start his own business, which, with the help of the Saudi oil boom of the seventies, became the Olayan Group still operating today.[8]

My own story of Suliman Olayan began with a call from a college classmate and friend, Joseph Farsoun, asking for a simple favor. After graduation, Joe had found a job with Arabian Commercial Enterprise, an insurance brokerage firm owned by Suliman. I had never met Suliman, but I had heard from friends about his legendary rise as a successful businessman. My first encounter was on one of my visits to Joe's office. Suliman happened to be there.

I tried to excuse myself for interrupting, but Suliman insisted that I come in. After a brief chat, he invited me to stop by his office sometime to visit with him. Weeks passed until, one day in July of 1968, Joe called me. "Mr. Olayan wants to see you. Could you stop by?" Joe had no idea why, and neither did I. And I could never anticipate the effect this phone call would have on my career, and life.

We met over a cup of coffee in his office on Hamra Street. The office reflected his reputation for modesty. He wore a suit and dress shirt with a necktie and spoke English with an American accent. While his secretary Hind took our coffee order, I couldn't help but notice the photos proudly displayed on the wall. One showed the ID badge—number forty—issued to him by his very first employer, Arabian American Oil Company. ARAMCO and Suliman had both come a long way. Another showed him in front of a giant off-highway Mack truck, transporting pipes for the Trans-Arabian pipeline. The last one was of Suliman standing in front of a simple store in downtown Alkhobar, with a Goodyear Tire sign above the shop entrance.

It took me a few minutes to get settled in his office, and when I started to feel more at ease, Suliman inundated me with a barrage of questions: about my background, education, my job as budget director at AUB. I mentioned my work in Riyadh, as part of the Ford Foundation's public administration reform project for the Saudi government. Suliman nodded, indicating his familiarity with the Saudi project, but sounded like he wanted to hear more, so I carried on. I probably spoke longer than he wanted, and he signaled with his index finger, indicating that he had heard enough. People who knew him told me later that this was his way of saying, *Let's get to the point.*

So we did.

"Samir, I wonder if you can help me?" he said. "My daughter is finishing high school this year. She applied for admission to AUB. Do you think you can help? I would like you just to check and let me know if she is qualified to join next year's freshman class. Otherwise I need to look early for a place in the US."

"I'm not sure how much I can help, but I will try to find out," I replied.

I was pleasantly surprised that a Saudi father, who was so involved with his business, was ready to dedicate time to the college education of his daughter. College education was normally reserved for male children. But he was keen not only to get her into college but into one of good standing. I left the meeting filled with respect for such an unusual, progressive father.

The next day, during my daily routine at AUB, I stopped in at the president's office a few minutes early for our daily cabinet meeting. I mentioned to Dr. Kirkwood that I had met Suliman Olayan the day before and that he had asked me for help. "Suliman wants to know whether his daughter is qualified for admission," I told him.

"Let me talk to Farid," Dr. Kirkwood replied. After he got off the phone with AUB's registrar, he turned to me and said, "That young lady is more than qualified to join the freshman class. She needs no special help from anyone."

Back in my office, I called Suliman and relayed to him what the registrar had said. He was extremely thankful and appreciated my effort. This was the beginning of a long-lasting relationship with Suliman, and later his son Khalid, first as friends and later as an executive in the group.

In this brief encounter, Suliman's warmth and charming personality made an impression on me. He was someone that any person might enjoy getting to know.

After that first meeting in 1968, Suliman came to Beirut quite often, and he called when he was in town. I would visit his office, and we would discuss business and economic growth in Saudi Arabia. He was always keen to share stories about his company's success. He talked about how in his early days he used his General Contracting Company as a vehicle for conducting business in Saudi Arabia. It was through this company that he built a close relationship of mutual trust and respect with the Bechtel family.

The growth in his business was due to the rapid expansion of the oil industry. "It's not enough to watch the growth and celebrate," he said. "We have to use this growth to build solid ground for the short- and long-term interests of the enterprise," he said. "We need to have the vision and guts to harness such openings."

On one of my following visits to Suliman's office, he brought up a topic that caught me by surprise—the need to hire senior people to help him in running his business.

"Samir, our businesses are growing," he said to me. "We need good people. Would you consider joining us?"

I didn't know what to say. At the time, I was happy with my position at AUB and wasn't looking to change jobs. But I offered to check with friends from among my AUB graduating class, if he wanted me to.

"That's good," he said. "Still, I'd like you to think about working for us even on a part-time basis. That could give you a chance to familiarize yourself with our business and see if it was something you'd like to do full time. Could you work after your AUB hours?"

It didn't take me too long to say yes and start wearing a new hat along with AUB's.

12
A Business Career in Turbulent Times

When AUB decided that they could not pursue healthcare consulting as a funding prospect, I had a gut feel that I should pursue it myself. Inspired by the success stories of businesses in the region, I thought this could be an opportunity, too. The firm's objective would be to create healthcare consulting in the Middle East. I quickly realized I was missing three essential elements. I had no time to spare, no capital to invest, and I knew of no reputable healthcare consulting firm that could provide the service. With friends, I went ahead to raise capital and register a company in Beirut. I hoped to find a joint venture partner, preferably from the US, since skills and technical know-how were more available in the US and Europe.

This concept had been successful in a variety of fields, like engineering, construction, defense and telecommunications. In this model, the role of the Middle East partner was to provide legal presence and knowledge, help secure contracts and interact with clients, something we could help provide. In Saudi Arabia prior to 2005, when the country joined the World Trade Organization, foreign companies were prevented by regulations from operating without a local partner or sponsor.

Finding a foreign partner in healthcare was one more challenge. I turned to a friend at the University of California. He recommended Herman Smith Associates, a reputable company he thought might be interested in a joint venture to offer services in the region. Herman Smith, a medical doctor, having started offering healthcare consulting in 1947, had been in the field for nearly twenty-five years. This sounded like a good fit, so I wrote to a senior partner there, providing him with information about opportunities in the Gulf region.

Ten days later, I received a discouraging letter from Leon Pullen. He said, "I discussed this opportunity with my partners. They thought it was too early to venture into international deals; the firm is very busy in the United States." But not long after, Leon wrote me again. "I like the idea personally and am ready to support it," he said. "Incidentally, my wife and I are planning a trip to London next week. I would be happy to meet with you guys and discuss your ideas."

I couldn't get away to go to London, so two of my partners met with him, and the meeting went well. They agreed to meet again at the Herman Smith Associates headquarters in Hinsdale, Illinois. In 1972, we signed a joint venture (JV) agreement. In this JV, one of our partners became general manager, and we formed a board with representatives from each side.

Although they had declined my first contact, our persistence and the convincing market data we provided helped change their outlook. Many US corporations were satisfied with sticking to doing business solely in the domestic market, with little ambition to discover what opportunities existed in the outside world. It took one Herman Smith partner with an entrepreneurial spirit to recognize the opportunity and convince his partners.

This attitude of looking outward has helped US corporations reap billions of dollars in the Gulf area. In the last twenty years, many mega projects have been awarded to US companies. Those projects contributed handsomely to corporations and the US economy.

Putting the JV together was the easy part. The real challenge, securing large projects, was more difficult than I expected. Hospital management firms, such as American Hospital Management and Humana, had advantages in scale and scope, and they had brand recognition. We had the brand but not the financial or human resources to undertake large-scale projects. Yet, we would succeed with smaller projects in Amman, Jordan.

It took several years before we procured a first contract—a three-year agreement, with an extension clause—with King Abdulaziz University in Jeddah to build and manage a temporary prefabricated 300-bed teaching hospital.

~

Our attempts to pursue business opportunities in the Middle East came at a delicate time when the region seemed to be spiraling out of control. The 1975 Lebanese civil war divided the country into Muslims fighting Christians, Lebanese fighting Palestinians, with the United States and France assuming a peacekeeping role. Several sad atrocities have stuck in my mind to this day.

One was in Ain el-Rammaneh, a Beirut suburb controlled by Christian militias. On Easter Sunday 1975, a bus loaded with Palestinian militia members from an Iraqi faction was crossing to a nearby refugee camp. The bus was hijacked and over twenty-five people massacred. Many Lebanese historians consider this as the spark that ignited the civil war.

I happened to be in the area, driving my parents to visit an uncle. We were caught in the chaos, with bullets flying everywhere. Deeply shaken but out of harm's way, I dropped off my parents and managed to navigate a safe return, thank God, to our home in Ras Beirut. This "tit-for-tat" killing and hostage taking continued in Lebanon and spread across the region.

A second atrocity took place in September of 1982. The Sabra and Shatila[9] massacre is a scar in the memories of Palestinians. It involved the killing of civilians, mostly Palestinians and Lebanese Shiites, by a right-wing party instructed by the Israeli Defense Forces to rid the camps of the Palestine Liberation Organization as part of its maneuver to occupy West Beirut.

The 1983 bombing of the US Marine barracks in Beirut was another act of brutality in this vicious civil war. The attack killed 220 marines. A nearby simultaneous explosion took the lives of fifty-eight French soldiers.

Economic stability, safety, security and the constitutional rule of law are essential to good business. The civil war forced many companies and individuals to leave the city for places out of harm's way. It affected AUB, as well. From the start of the conflict, the PLO took control of West Beirut, which included the campus, the hospital, the American Embassy and the adjacent area of Ras Beirut. It also provided security to those facilities, guarding them from other more militant Palestinian factions.

For the most part, the campus stayed calm. But on February 17, 1976, after starting as an ordinary day of classes, AUB became anything but calm. By the end of the day, a student gunman had killed two faculty members. The assailant, Najem Najem, a twenty-three-year-old Jordanian engineering student, was one of more than a hundred students—mostly Palestinians—whom AUB had expelled the year before for strikes and sit-ins. That morning, he returned to campus holding a pistol and several hand grenades. He gunned down the dean of engineering, Raymond Ghosn, who died in the hospital. He then shot to death the dean of students Robert Najemi. He ran across campus to the main administration building and went straight to the third floor, searching for the university president, Samuel B. Kirkwood.

I found myself in a lockdown situation in the office of the university provost in College Hall, next to the office of the president. I had been meeting with staff members, including the provost. Fortunately, the provost received a phone call that probably saved our lives, informing him of the killings and warning him to lock and stay inside his office. While Najem was searching for the university president, security helped Kirkwood slip out of the building during the confusion.

Najem attempted to break into the provost's office. Only that door stood between us and certain death—but by then it was tightly locked. Najem moved on and entered the office of University Vice President George Hakim, taking him hostage at gunpoint along with eight other staff members, among them Radwan Mawlawi, director of communications, who was allowed to leave the group to act as a mediator. The deadlock continued for a tense hour.

We remained locked in the provost's office, receiving phone updates from the head of security. To release the hostages, Najem demanded a car with a driver. A medical professor and later Lebanon's minister of education, Dr. Najib Abu Haydar, assisted in the mediation. He offered himself as a hostage instead of Dr. George Hakim, the primary target in the group of nine captives. Najem refused the trade, but Abu Haydar's courageous efforts, with the help of the Fatah faction of the Palestinian militias, succeeded in ending the crisis without the deaths of any more AUB faculty. During the operation, Najem was shot and killed.

The turbulence of the mid-seventies affected AUB in many ways. We were forced to announce a hike in tuition and fees, a move that we managed to couple with an increase in scholarships. Anti-American sentiment had grown among students following Arab defeats in two wars against Israel. And some of our students were taking part in commando training camps. Students focused on a tuition increase as an excuse, and their leaders threatened AUB with radical measures, followed by an open strike, at the same time occupying College Hall and several other university buildings. In the end, the administration retracted the tuition increase, which helped ease the situation and brought students back to their classes.

Media coverage of these events in the US affected our reputation as an American institution of higher education. AUB was subject to harsh criticism from Israeli officials, who saw AUB as a breeding ground for liberal ideas that fed an ideology opposed to the long-term interests of Israel.

Dr. Kirkwood's presidency was a trying time for him, and AUB. To his credit, he struggled to keep AUB open during such devastating circumstances. He cultivated alums, especially from Arab Gulf countries, to raise badly needed funds to replace what was lost in USAID funding. I accompanied him on some of those fruitful visits, along with the team from the development office.

That day in February 1976 opened my eyes to the impact of the Lebanese civil war and its security challenges for AUB. A dozen years later, on January 18, 1984, I was reminded of that earlier tragic day by the news coming out of Beirut about AUB President Malcolm Kerr. Reports confirmed that he was fatally shot twice in the head by two gunmen in front of his office. His death became international headlines. Much of Kerr's life had been spent in the Mideast and at AUB—his parents had taught there for forty years, and he spent much of his youth in Beirut.

Kerr graduated from Princeton, became a professor and dean at UCLA, and eventually returned to AUB as a professor before being named president. Three of his four children were born in Beirut, including son Steve, the well-known former Chicago Bulls player and current basketball coach of the Golden State Warriors. Steve Kerr does not hesitate to speak openly and humanly about the history and politics of the Mideast, with a depth of knowledge born of experience and loss. He could have been speaking for his father when, in December 2016, he told a *New York Times* reporter:

> It's really simple to demonize Muslims because of our anger over 9/11, but it's obviously so much more complex than that. The vast majority of Muslims are peace-loving people, just like the vast majority of Christians and Buddhists and Jews and any other religion. People are people.

Malcolm Kerr would have been proud of his son's compassionate courage and forgiveness.

13
CIVIL WAR AND ESCAPE FROM BEIRUT

In early 1976, the security situation in Beirut was deteriorating rapidly. Rocket fire was being exchanged between the eastern Christian part of Beirut and the western sector, controlled by Palestinian militias and their Lebanese allies. AUB was directly in the line of fire. The US State Department issued advisories, alerting citizens about visiting or staying in Lebanon. The fighting forced the Beirut Airport Authority to close the airport indefinitely. Foreign embassies began to prepare for the evacuation of their citizens on ships from the Beirut seaport to Cyprus, which became the staging point for the return of evacuees to their home countries. AUB faculty and staff, especially Americans, heeded the advice and began moving with their families out of the war zone.

When AUB's vice president of administration, John Gill, called me in March of 1976, I was surprised to hear of his plans to leave for the US for several weeks. In the meantime, I would fill in for him until his return. John noticed my hesitation. Was I the right person to do this job with so much responsibility—a *Palestinian* in Lebanon, in the midst of a civil war?

With reservations, I accepted the temporary assignment.

In John's absence, I worked directly with the president and had to be available at all times. Dr. Kirkwood was conscious of the dangers surrounding the campus and keen to ensure we did what was necessary to protect our students, faculty and staff, and safeguard the campus and Medical Center from harm. Every morning, the president's cabinet, including deans and administrative officers, met for updates on the latest events and developments, both on and outside the campus.

West Beirut was already under the control of Palestinian militias and their supporters. Militia leaders were pressuring AUB to give them access to the campus. They wanted us to provide them with water and electricity—the first of many requests. City electricity and water were being rationed. AUB had its own power generators and water sources. After consultation with Dr. Kirkwood, the head of campus security responded: "We cannot grant anyone access to, or share, any of our utilities."

It was distressing for all of us to have to guard the university, a place of peace and learning, against the encroachment of military factions.

However, the AUB Medical Center was crucial to militias of both sides, as they both needed medical services. And this, we felt we could not deny them. Using the medical services as leverage, we were able to defuse the situation amicably, in return for a promise that the militias would protect the campus and Medical Center. This same group of militias provided similar help to the US Embassy, located close to the AUB lower campus.

The civil war brought with it total disruption affecting AUB in multiple ways—campus security, medical supplies, safe passage for students, faculty or patients, banking services. At one point, the University's bank, HSBC, notified our chief accountant, Mr. Haikal, that they couldn't continue processing the university payroll. In response, Mr. Haikal asked the bank to deliver cash in a secure vehicle to campus. The bank agreed, and we sent out word to faculty and staff to get to the cashier's office quickly to collect their salaries.

At home, Abla and I had to shield our apartment from shrapnel and broken glass. We both realized that our remaining time in Beirut was short when one quiet day in March 1976 the silence was shattered by a whistling sound—followed by a loud explosion. Shrapnel landed on the balcony where, minutes earlier, Ramez had been riding his tricycle. Now the war was in our midst. We moved the wardrobe from the kids' bedroom to cover the sliding glass door to the balcony. That night, shrapnel shattered that same door. We decided to limit our movements to the corridor, where there were two cement walls on either side, just in case. In that hallway, we placed two mattresses.

Our friends Akram Hijazi, his wife Nawar, their baby Asseel and Nawar's father took refuge in our apartment because their house had no safe area. The eight of us slept sideways on the mattresses in our hallway, just as my siblings and I had done when we first fled Jaffa for Beirut, and throughout the night we learned the sounds of war. If a rocket whistled, we knew it was close and would either hit our house or explode down the road. Whenever we heard that whistling sound, we took deep breaths and waited for the explosion.

During a lull in the fighting, Akram and his family moved to Greece. There he joined his teammates from the Olayan Group who had moved their headquarters from Beirut to Athens.

In late June 1976, the American Embassy called Abla, advising her to ready the family for evacuation at any time. She and I spent the last couple of weeks preparing a shipment of valued belongings, especially those that had sentimental value. Packing kept us busy when the electric power went out. We consolidated our shipment with one for another family member shipping to the same California address. When our landlord heard about our plans to leave, he offered to buy all our furniture and fixtures—lucky for us.

Then we expectantly awaited the US embassy's evacuation order to board the ship that would take Americans and their families to Cyprus, and from there to the United States. We waited and waited, until finally we learned that the ship had come and gone. It had forgotten us.

Anxiously, we called the American Embassy. After many apologies, the staff person told us that the embassy would arrange for us to join a German convoy that was heading by land to Syria. We were instructed to secure a vehicle and rendezvous at a place where we could join the convoy.

On the day prior to our departure, I walked to the taxi office to book and pay for a pickup early the next morning to drive us to Damascus. Abla got all the things we needed for the boys and ourselves ready. The next morning, the taxi never came. Abla and I ran down the street, from one corner to another, searching for a taxi. After what seemed like hours, a taxi stopped. We explained our dilemma to the driver. He was already booked. But he knew someone who would drive us.

Off we went in his taxi, to the sound of bullets, unable to put out of mind the kidnappings going on in Beirut. But this honorable man drove us to his friend, who agreed to drive us to Damascus. Then he drove us home, where my parents had been taking care of four-year-old Ramez and two-year-old Ziad.

Despite the fighting all around us, my parents could not and did not want to leave Beirut. They had no visas to travel with and, living in West Beirut, were surrounded by other displaced Palestinians like ourselves who had flocked to the district as a refuge. They couldn't bear to be uprooted again but were relieved that we could get out and get their grand-children away from the fighting.

Saying goodbye to my heartbroken parents filled me with sadness and regret. It was another wrenching separation that cut deeply but that I couldn't afford to stop and acknowledge at the time.

We picked up the children and luggage, and headed to the rendezvous area to join the German convoy. After we regis-tered our names with an embassy staff, he asked us to stay with the convoy until we reached our destination. Our driver was pleasant but impatient. He began passing one car, then another. After a time, our car was traveling alone, no convoy to be seen. We kept silent, fearing the driver might abandon us in the middle of the road somewhere.

Finally, at a crowded, noisy Syrian border, we cleared our passports. Still there was no sign of the German convoy. So we headed to the American Embassy, our meeting point in

Damascus. Appropriately, it was Sunday, July 4th. The doors were open and they were expecting us. Luckily, Tom Ball, the USAID officer in the Beirut embassy, whom I knew from AUB, was meeting the convoy. He said all the hotels were filled except for two rooms in one of the cheap hotels, and he directed us there.

Fortunately, Abla had packed disinfectant and went about cleaning whatever in the room the boys might touch. It was noisy at night because the hotel staff had put mattresses in the hallways for people to sleep on. When we finally secured our plane tickets for a flight to Frankfurt, then to San Francisco, the Damascus airport was in total chaos. With the Beirut airport closed due to heavy bombardment by Lebanese forces, all Beirut passengers had been diverted to Syrian airports. Having kids helped us clear the long lines at the airline desks and at immigration. Abla and I, our hands clasped tightly together, realized, *This time is for real. No return for sure.*

We landed in San Francisco to an emotional reunion with Abla's parents, my sister and her family. Ramez and Ziad gave their grandparents unspeakable joy. I looked at Abla. With tears in her eyes, she said, "A new chapter in our life."

My days at AUB, as a student and on the staff, had been among the precious years in my life and my family's. We would always remember days we took the kids to play on the campus, with its beautiful view of the Mediterranean and of snow-capped Mount Sunnin, and would treasure the friendships we made there.

In Berkeley, we lived with Abla's parents while we looked for a home we could afford. Our means were limited—working so long for nonprofit organizations wasn't necessarily the best way to save money. So living temporarily with them made us feel at home, and we regained a sense of peace we had been missing in Beirut. We stayed with them for nine months until a condominium became available in Albany, adjacent to Berkeley, which we were able to get thanks to a loan from Abla's father and an uncle who insisted on helping us.

A few days after our arrival in Berkeley, Loren Furtado, my colleague at the University of California, had called. "Glad you all arrived safely. I have a job lined up for you. Take a month's rest, get settled and we will talk about the job later." Loren and his wife Mary were true friends. Caring people who helped get us settled in the East Bay, they both were always there and ready to help, a kindness for which Abla and I would be forever grateful.

We followed Loren's advice to relax, taking the boys on trips around the Bay Area. Life started to look and feel better again, and we settled into our new world. Ramez could attend a nearby nursery school. Abla found a job with California Savings Bank, while Ziad stayed with his grandmother during the day, and I started my job at the UC system. It was at a lower job grade than my position at AUB, which reminded me of what happened to my father when we moved to Beirut. But my mother's words to my father kept ringing in my ears: "Issa, nothing is beneath you when you need to earn a living." What was important was that I had a job, thanks to Loren, and that we had a welcoming home with Abla's parents.

Deep down, I knew that this would not be a repeat of what my parents had to go through when they left Palestine in 1948. I was really touched by how wonderful Abla's parents were. Their house became our house. We were comforted by how generous, caring and loving a family could be. For that we remain forever grateful.

As it does to this day, UC Berkeley enjoyed a worldwide reputation as a cradle of scholarship and progressive ideas. My cohorts in the budget office gave me a warm welcome. One member of the staff, an African American named George Jackson, was particularly considerate. He was aware of my Palestinian background and had good knowledge about the Middle East and the Palestinian strife. Originally from Madison, Georgia, during his high school and college years he had been active in the civil rights movement. He joined peaceful marches that often ended with police and white supremacists attacking the marchers. He told me the Palestinian struggle was no different than theirs. He spoke proudly about the struggle of African Americans and their achievements but was skeptical about the future, if change didn't continue.

My other colleagues were kind to include me in their coffee breaks and lunches. Still, I often felt like an outsider. I didn't have a favorite football team and was clueless about internal Berkeley city politics or office gossip. The things constantly on my mind in my Mediterranean world were the Middle East and the Palestinian-Israeli conflict, the last things on theirs.

The job itself was not too demanding and left me with time to start work on my master's degree. I registered in an evening program at Golden Gate University in San Francisco and eventually graduated with an MBA. I still remember the nightly commute to San Francisco's Market Street to attend classes—crossing the Bay Bridge, getting to the University and searching for a parking spot as a newcomer to the city.

Attending graduate school was an invaluable experience. As an adult with many years of work experience, it helped bring together things I was learning in the classroom with what I had learned in the workplace. Although I sometimes asked myself why I had returned to school again at this point in my life, the reason was always the same. It was a lesson I had diligently internalized since when we became refugees in 1948—in striving for a better life, your best chance is to pin your hopes on education.

In mid-1977 I received an unexpected call from a man named Aziz Syriani. "I'm in San Francisco, at the Sheraton Hotel. Mr. Suliman Olayan asked me to introduce myself. What is your schedule tomorrow?" We agreed to meet the next morning.

At that time, Aziz was a senior advisor to the Olayan Group. The first thing we talked about was the civil war and how he had been forced to bring his family to Athens. We both wondered whether the war in Lebanon was a continuation of traumatic events started in Palestine in 1948 or a sad, new chapter for the region.

Aziz came with a message from Mr. Olayan. He wanted me to consider joining his group in Athens. The job was internal group auditor. While appreciative of the offer, with some hesitation I said, "I'm not keen on the audit field and don't have the right experience. But if something else comes along, yes, I would be delighted. Please thank him for thinking of me."

When first living in the US, as a permanent resident or visitor, you may feel excited and exhilarated by the country's magic and novelty. I had heard lots of stories from family members and friends about how this novelty wears off. They confided to me about their struggle to adjust to life in the US. Many experienced culture shock, anxiety, disorientation that comes from the difficulty of assimilating into a very different culture. In my case, it was a big adjustment dealing with work, social relationships and daily life. Though my arrival in the US was a result of a desperate situation in Lebanon, many times I found myself idealizing life back at AUB—missing my job, the pride I took in what I did there, my self-esteem. In my job at UC, I didn't see much chance for advancement.

One day another unexpected call came, this time from Leon Pullen, our partner from Herman Smith. He spoke about difficulties they were facing with the King Abdulaziz University Hospital management project, including hiring a chief financial officer. He wanted to know if I would consider moving to Saudi Arabia and taking this job for a year until they filled the position permanently.

I asked him, "What do I do when the year is over?"

"You can come work for Herman Smith in the US," he said.

14
A Job in Saudi

Since 1948, our life had been transient, roaming from place to place. Despite the fact that I had been able to attend college and work in the field of higher education, that I had gained identity cards as a student and employee, had even become a US citizen, at heart I felt displaced. My parents had taught me, from the day my feet touched the ground in Lebanon that survival and bettering yourself meant making sacrifices, like being separated from the people and things you valued most. Tying your life to a place, to an emotion or memories, to your people and history—all proved hurtful. I saw little choice but to numb myself. Self-denial was a price I chose to pay, instead of living life to the fullest with what I had.

It was difficult to decide whether or not to accept the job offer with Herman Smith in Saudi Arabia. Three years had already passed since we had left Beirut. Slowly, we had settled in to our small, two-bedroom condominium with a view of the Golden Gate Bridge. The kids were in school, and Abla had a part-time job at the Bank of California. We were near Abla's family and my sister. What prompted me to consider the new position?

Abla and I talked it over. I wanted to be able to provide security for our family and educational chances for our children that my current nonprofit job might not lead to. Also, my job at UC made me wish for work that was more challenging and meaningful, that might even make a difference in the region I was from. There was always in me a refugee's persistent fear of failure and a desire to excel, to make something more out of myself and my circumstances.

Abla and I agreed to make no commitment until I had a chance to visit Jeddah and learn more about the living conditions and details of the position.

I spent several days in Jeddah, toured the teaching hospital and spoke with dedicated doctors and staff members, predominantly Saudi nationals. It was a brand-new temporary hospital of three hundred beds with outpatient and medical clinics, all prefabricated modules with state-of-the-art medical equipment. Herman Smith hired the nursing staff, all of whom came from outside Saudi Arabia and virtually from the four corners of the earth.

My two big concerns were schooling for the children and housing. I visited the American School in Jeddah, offering classes from K to 12. The school was run along the lines of the US school system. Plus it offered small classes with teachers geared to educating expatriate children. Management assured me they would find suitable housing.

Abla and I decided to take the risk, accept the offer and tell the kids.

Ramez was seven years old at the time. One morning when I was taking him to school, I told him we were moving to Saudi Arabia. He had no idea of where Saudi was. He only remembered sounds of fighting and shattered glass in Beirut. He asked me, "Will we ever come back?" I told him that this would always be home for us. This was where his grandparents and our family were. With tears in his eyes, he looked at me and said, "OK." He reminded me of myself in April 1948 when I left my home in Jaffa. But this time we would all be traveling as a family, with US passports, as US citizens. Now we would always have a place to return to.

After having been in the States for three years, in December 1979 I took the oath of US citizenship at a courthouse in San Francisco near Union Square with at least a hundred others. After administering the oath of citizenship, the judge instructed us: "Don't let anyone tell you that you are any less a citizen just because you're the newest. We're pretty much all refugees here. It's just a question of when we arrived." The judge's words lifted a heavy weight from my shoulders, and I felt a wave of relief and immense pride.

As I expected, the demand for housing in Saudi was high. The arrival of large numbers of US and European expatriates, with their families, made the situation more difficult. Abla and I agreed that she and the boys would stay in Amman for a time, and I would commute to Jeddah by plane to work and look for housing. Abla and the boys stayed in a hotel in Amman for the next two months, and we registered Ramez in kindergarten at the American Community School in Amman. Luckily, we had good friends in the city, Tuma and Renee Yaghnam, who could help care for Abla and the kids while I was away.

After several months of searching, a small three-bedroom house became available in Jeddah. This became our home.

King Abdulaziz University Hospital's administrative system faced many challenges during my time there. I drew on my experience at AUB to find solutions to problems and gained the confidence and friendship of many of the Saudi physicians. The Saudi staff doctors had great talent and energy, and were keen to serve. Among them was Dr. Usama Shobokshi, who became dean of the medical faculty at the university, then university president and, for several terms, Saudi minister of health. He brought discipline, transparency, honesty and integrity to all of his leadership roles, and we would remain good friends. People like him deserve credit for modernizing Saudi Arabia's healthcare system.

The most gratifying aspect of the work was bringing experience and knowledge I had acquired in my career to a teaching hospital that needed basic principles of fiscal control. Issuing a procurement order or a payment voucher, even keeping a basic ledger—these were unheard of before the Herman Smith project began. The hospital badly needed operating systems to deliver services successfully. It was meaningful to know that, in a modest way, I was helping one hospital in my home region acquire sorely needed management tools, and it made the move to Jeddah seem worth the risks and uncertainty.

Our family life in Jeddah was made a bit easier thanks to the American Embassy. We had access to the grounds to swim or play tennis. Abla and the kids spent time there after school or on school holiday breaks. There, in the pool, one of the kids asked Ramez where he was from. He said, "Well, I don't really know. I'm kind of American, kind of Palestinian and kind of Lebanese."

I wondered about the impact that our nomadic lifestyle would have on our sons. Would they suffer from not having a strong sense of identity tied to a homeland? Would they always feel like immigrants wherever they went? In the end, I think our frequent moves during their early lives helped them become global citizens, learning that people everywhere are the same, regardless of what language they speak.

In 1979, while I was on a business trip to Al Khobar, Saudi Arabia, I phoned Suliman Olayan's son Khalid, whom I had not seen in some time. I wanted to introduce him to a colleague of mine from Herman Smith Associates, Richard Wittrup. Khalid called back and said, "Yes, let's get together. We have a board meeting in Al Khobar. Some of your good friends will be here. I'm sure they would love to see you."

I enjoyed the visit with Khalid and his colleagues. The next day he called me.

"I spoke to my father. He wonders if you would be interested in joining our group. We are looking for a new president of Olayan Financing Company. The current president wanted to return home to the United States."

This sounded like a good match and opportunity. "Let's meet and talk about it more," I replied.

"Aziz Syriani will contact you soon," he said.

Aziz appears in my life again, I thought to myself.

Olayan Financing Company (OFC) was an independent entity that managed joint ventures with companies like Bechtel, Nitro Noble and General Dynamics, and invested in Saudi manufacturing and industrial enterprises. The idea of this job appealed to me. I felt I could communicate well with, and add value to, partners and others in developing new businesses.

The next week, we met again and agreed on terms of employment. I would start in August 1980, the beginning of the school year for our sons at the American Academy, in Dhahran.

But several weeks later, Aziz called unexpectedly. "Samir, we have a change in plan." He informed me that I was needed in the Group's trading and distribution businesses.

I was baffled by this quick change of mind, but it was too late for me to turn down the offer. I had already told my partners in Jeddah that I was leaving.

During my first few weeks on the job, it became apparent that my previous work in academic institutions and consulting did not prepare me for work in a trade and distribution environment, especially in Saudi Arabia. Everything about the position was different than what I had done in my previous jobs. After almost a year, I spoke to Khalid Olayan about leaving. He was disappointed and suggested I try a bit longer, which I did.

When Khalid Olayan was still quite young, his mother passed away. As he was growing up, he developed a special relationship with his uncle Abdullah, Suliman's brother. His uncle reinforced in him their family's values of modesty, honesty and loyalty, and Khalid demonstrated these traits time and again in all his dealings. Khalid's hand was close to his country's pulse, which gave him a unique, matchless local understanding among his peers in the Group. He was proud to be part of an Arab group, built by Arabs, adhering to the best practices and highest ethical standards among local and international business enterprises.

After a two-year stint with the Saudi Ministry of Finance, Khalid joined the Olayan Group. He worked closely with his archetypal entrepreneur father, who wanted to instill in him his own value system. Khalid built a successful career in the Group, and after his father's passing in 2003, he took on the key role as chairman. In that role, he sustained the integrity of the organization and his father's legacy, while management was handled by his two remarkable sisters, Hutham and Lubna. I have witnessed with great admiration how this Middle East family business group successfully transformed itself into a global entity, while retaining its family culture. Credit for the success of this business model is due to Aziz Syriani, who knew how to keep the pieces of the mosaic held tightly together.

Now when I look back to my early association with the Group, I believe I made the wrong choice by accepting the trading and distribution position. The Olayan Finance Company would have been a better fit for me.

Late in 1982 I decided that I should move on. Fortunately at that time, I was offered another position with the group, in London, as assistant to the chairman.

With fingers crossed, I accepted.

15
LONDON

From Saudi Arabia, we flew directly to London and began our search for an apartment and a school for the boys. We had no luck finding a place to live but were able to enroll our sons in the American School of London. Khalid Akhrass, a colleague and a good friend from the Olayan office in London, volunteered to help us in our search for a place to live while we returned to Berkeley for the summer. We were relieved when he called us to say he had found an apartment, flat number 4 at 17 Cheney Gardens. He said, "I put down a small deposit that will hold it until you get here."

I was delighted to have our living situation settled, and I happily signed a one-year lease. That evening, I called Abla. "Time to pack. We have a place to live."

Abla and our sons loved the three-bedroom flat, a nice place in a neighborhood close to the embankment.

The move to London gave me frequent opportunities to work directly with Suliman Olayan, as he was generous in providing time and support for me to succeed. This led to the most gratifying experience in my entire association with the Group ever since this relationship first started, back at our first meeting in his office in Beirut in 1968, and which then lasted for several decades. Being in London gave me a chance to get to know him as a businessman and to learn first-hand about the keys to his success. I came to appreciate the reasons why he was so admired and respected.

In this new association, I discovered a person who loved the livelihood of business for its own sake and who never allowed power or wealth to make him forget his humble beginnings. He retained all the positive traits of Saudis, traits that have sustained a people through the harshness of desert life: survival, patience, loyalty and faith. He exuded a persistent curiosity to acquire and share knowledge, a thirst that remained with him until the waning days of his life. Within himself he integrated his roots as a Saudi Arab with a professional acumen acquired from his interactions with global business and political leaders, a combination of qualities that reflected the best of both worlds.

Suliman was particularly proud of creating an Arab enterprise of international stature, but his business ethic set a high bar for executives and employees, especially family members. Unlike a number of Arab companies that have seen meteoric rises and falls over the last few decades, the Group has withstood the tests of time and still stands on sold ground.

The Olayan Group was staffed by Palestinians, Lebanese, Syrians, Jordanians, mostly college graduates, all assuming senior positions that were instrumental in building the group's foundation. "On this journey I never intended—or ever intend—to give up my Arab identity," he said. "I want to build a company that can hold to the best standards of ethics and business practices, but remain an Arab Group we all can be proud of." I heard this theme repeatedly on many occasions during his lifetime.

Every time I see an Arab organization targeted and torn down, I remind myself of his words, which still ring in my ears. For the last seventy years, the Arab region has been living through conflict and violence, wars that have destroyed structures of brick and mortar, and the lives and livelihoods of millions of people, while undermining safety and security. Nothing remains safe, including the economies that sustain life. Since 1948, Palestinian institutions have been targeted, but seemingly endless conflict throughout the region has undermined the possibility of social progress.

Arab countries have been unable to defend themselves on the battlefield and today are incapable of safeguarding their wealth and resources. They continue to pay a heavy price in internal strife, a consequence of greedy interventions by foreign powers. Iraq, Syria, Egypt, the Gulf states, Saudi Arabia, Lebanon—in one way or another, all face these types of dangers each day.

Intra Bank was founded in Lebanon in 1951 by Palestinian Banker Yousuf Beidas, "the Genius from Jerusalem." For a time it was a great success story, but it later suffered a disastrous financial collapse. The Arab Bank was founded in Jerusalem in 1930. The US Treasury Department forced it to close its US branches. Likewise, Arabia Insurance was started in Jerusalem by Basim Faris, a 1931 Harvard Business School graduate. The company for years ranked high among insurance companies in the region. Now it struggles to survive. Balanced economic development in the Middle East seems like a fairy tale, as war-weary countries desperately seek to rebuild their industries and regain foreign investment to stave off the devastation of economic collapse and stanch the slide into mass poverty.

The region's enemies zoom in on its economies, as susceptible to attack as any military targets. Other than the few nations possessing an abundance of natural resources, Arab peoples throughout the region struggle to achieve the successes they once dreamt possible.

I watched Suliman expend tireless effort to correct biases against Arabs and Palestinians, which elements of the US government, media and think tanks find so difficult to reject. In the US and the West, media coverage of Saudi Arabia, in particular, could give more attention to the country's cultural heritage and complexity, and life seen through the eyes of its ordinary people.

Sometimes Suliman felt as though he was alone in his crusade, but just as frequently he stood with likeminded progressive Arab businessmen: Hasib Sabbagh and Sa'id Khouri, founders of Consolidated Construction Company; Omar Aggad, prominent Saudi/Palestinian businessman; and former Lebanese prime minister Rafik Hariri.

Suliman understood Western attitudes and thinking, and could navigate both Western and Middle Eastern cultures. Unlike in many family companies in the Middle East, his children could join the Group only after they had completed graduate studies and gained experience through several years of outside work. There was no place for nepotism to override values and judgment. The integrity and continuity of the business enterprise was the top concern, ahead of family.

He derived strength by fostering the strengths of those around him, and their strengths became his. One time Suliman was introducing Akram Hijazi, the Group's chief financial officer and a member of the inner circle, to the chairman of a large bank. He was asked what made Akram special. "Ice water runs in his veins," he answered. This left the bank chair with a useful impression of the CFO, while boosting Hijazi's self-confidence and demonstrating Suliman's ability to identify and support talent.

I traveled many miles with Mr. Olayan, working on ventures with global companies. On these occasions, he consistently charmed those around him, whether a chairman from a large corporation or a prominent banker. I consider myself one of the lucky ones to have gotten a chance to know and work with him during my career with the Group.

There is good evidence that Olayan Group's second and third generation will honor Suliman's legacy, relying on Arab talent to sustain a steady commitment to the region and continuing to take pride in the Arab cultural heritage and identity despite internal skeptics, external influences and glossy temptations.

~

Directly above us in our London flat lived a Jewish family, the Gollances. Rodney Gollance was a scrap metal trader, a business he inherited from his father. One day his wife Julia visited Abla and noticed that most of our books were about Palestine and Israel. Abla explained our background and my interest in the conflict. Rodney turned out to be an avid reader, interested in this period in history. They kindly introduced us to London in a way only locals can. That included the Chelsea Flower Show, Hampton Court Music Festival, the Races at the Royal Ascot, Trooping the Color—a British and Commonwealth armies parade tradition since the seventeenth century—and the Henley Royal Regatta, an annual rowing event on the River Thames. The Gollances remain our close friends.

In the flat just below us lived Lord Robert Napier, fifth Baron of Magdala, who was a brigadier in the Royal Engineers. A frail gentleman in his mid-eighties, he was recording his memoir, recollecting events with the help of a graduate student. He was happy to have me listen in as he talked about the British occupation of Iraq, the revolution against the British occupation in the 1920s and the brutal British colonial forces that quelled the countrywide uprising through the use of air power. I enjoyed talking with him about the colonial era and the British and French rule following the collapse of the Ottoman Empire. These were glorious days for him as a Brit and sad ones for me as a Palestinian.

On our way back from dinner one freezing London night, with snow covering the roads, Abla and I noticed a group of photographers gathered in front of the building next door at 15 Cheney Gardens. "Those are paparazzi," Abla observed.

The glamorous target of their attention turned out to be Elizabeth Taylor, a neighbor we had never met. It became normal to see paparazzi hanging around the front door of that building, hoping that she would emerge or return to her flat when she was in town so they could score a scoop for the newspapers.

We enjoyed our apartment at Cheney Gardens for two years. Then we moved to Onslow Square, in South Kensington, to be close to an underground station, where the boys could more easily get to school.

Among the other happy aspects of the London move was the chance to reconnect with friends I had grown up with in Tripoli and Beirut. One dear friend, gifted Lebanese political cartoonist Mahmoud Kahil, had gained prominence, popularity and notoriety in his field. His insightful work satirized the totalitarian regimes and military dictators over-whelming the Middle East—and his best work was reserved for the Palestinian-Israeli conflict. He was a humane artist who couldn't help but side with the weak and the underdog, whether in the Middle East, Africa or other places around the world, regardless of ethnicity, race, religion or nationality. He drew fine pieces of many world leaders, including US presidents and Yasser Arafat, his most appealing caricature. Mahmoud's work appeared in the global press, as well as in his book, *According to Kahil*.

London offered Mahmoud a work environment where freedom of the press was respected. Not just a good friend, Mahmoud became a member of our family. Ramez and Ziad loved him as a second father, and he considered them his own. When reminiscing about good times in Beirut, he would talk about how difficult it was to be a political cartoonist depicting our part of the world, with threats and warnings coming from military regimes he dared to criticize.

One evening, when he arrived at our flat for dinner, he wasn't in his usual upbeat, joyful spirits. "I normally get phone calls from readers outside the UK who've enjoyed a caricature I've done," he said. "This time the caller wasn't an admirer. I suspect he belonged to an intelligence agency, and he was upset with my last cartoon. It depicts a dictator frantically trying to steer a sailboat through rough seas, with the wind refusing to cooperate. He called me 'Comrade Mahmoud' and said, 'Your caricature yesterday is filth. I'm warning you, next time we see anything about our leader, you won't have a hand to draw with.'"

This was the kind of pressure he had to resist.

He spent every Christmas Eve with us. When Christmas 2002 came around, Mahmoud called us to apologize that he wouldn't be able to come. "This year," he said, "I would like to go see my sister and her family." Sadly, early in 2003, he passed away from heart complications.

It is a sad loss that his professional journey ended so early. I'm sure he would have produced even more remarkable work, especially with the current chaotic situation in the Middle East. In the age of Trump, he would have been God's gift to political caricature.

We still miss Mahmoud, as do his many friends and admirers across the Arab world.

~

Even while being a parent, Abla always had learning on her mind, and in 1993 at age forty-four, when both our sons had gone to college, she registered at the American University in Richmond, now known as Richmond University, in London. She enrolled part-time in the psychology department and graduated three years later with highest distinction, summa cum laude, and gave the commencement speech for her class.

She enjoyed her time there and being challenged by her professors. When she came home, she would tell me stories about how the other students in class viewed her. At the beginning of every semester, as she walked into the classroom, students would turn around and sit up, thinking she was the professor. But as she took her seat among them, everyone relaxed.

After graduation, she applied to the one-year program in counseling at Regent's University London. After completing the program, she offered addiction and bereavement counseling.

~

My job responsibilities in London as an assistant to the chairman included external relations and groupwide business development. Yet, my duties were ambiguous, and I realized that it was up to me to make something out of the job this time. Three years in Saudi Arabia helped me understand the workings of a diversified group with multiple business lines —manufacturing, distribution, trading, logistics, construction —owned either solely or jointly with foreign partners who brought technical know-how to the Saudi market. Olayan himself was a pioneer in this field. He was the first Saudi businessman to recognize the benefits of joint ventures—he secured solid partnerships with Bechtel, Cummins engines, Kenworth trucks—a model later adopted by many businesses in the region.

Doing business in the Middle East presents challenges typical of developing economies. Often, they lack the legal structure, banking and financial services, organized public infrastructure, skilled professionals, transparency and—above all—political stability and security necessary to build a sustainable economy. Some developing nations struggle on all fronts, even to this day. Others, like Dubai, have broken the mold.

Working with the Group, I learned four golden rules for working with partners.

Business success depends on continually nurturing relationships.

Fairness and honesty are more important than outsmarting partners.

Short-term gain, without care, can turn into long-term pain.

No arms deals, no oil trading, no partnerships with bigwigs and no business with the tobacco industry.

Suliman learned these golden rules from his own experience and imbedded them in the company's corporate culture.

As founder, he strongly believed in working hard to earn a living. The portfolio focused on businesses that don't require political leverage. Manufacturing, distributing, consumer goods, soft drink bottling, hospital supplies, and selling heavy equipment were models of ones that could succeed without need for political influence.

He was a strong believer in communication. The distribution list of any communication had to be extensive. As a matter of habit, he would add missing names to any memo and send it back for redistribution. I'm sure that, in his mind, he believed that wide distribution increases the possibility of learning from more viewpoints and creating better dialogue. He had full-time staff in New York, London and Riyadh preparing daily reviews of the press and had it distributed to key personnel in the group. Always thirsty to learn, one time he asked me the meaning of an English word. I appeared hesitant, and he looked at me and said, "Samir, get the Webster's dictionary. We can learn a new word together."

London was an exceptional place to do business development for the Group. Being there put me in proximity to our partners. In the 1980s, the city attracted many US companies that wanted to open headquarters there for Europe, the Middle East and Africa. With a thorough knowledge of the Group business, I could anticipate future openings for new ventures and fill gaps to expand Group businesses.

The time I spent in Saudi Arabia had helped me understand that country's economy. My business education and experience helped me cross from the Middle East to Europe to America. Business partners were looking for compatible people who shared a similar sense of ethics, values and corporate culture. Our group met all the requirements.

Most importantly, being in London offered me close proximity to a remarkable mentor.

Suliman Olayan was a leader with a broad vision. Any time we signed an agreement with a new partner, he would encourage me to look for ways to expand the relationship within and beyond our region.

He led a modest life. He owned no mansions or yachts, maintained a low-profile lifestyle, and his business ethics earned him the respect and admiration of people locally and from around the world.

16

COCA-COLA AND THE ARAB-ISRAELI BOYCOTT

My recipe for success in my new job in London was simple. I figured that to excel and be recognized by my peers and employer, I needed to make a difference, to make positive contributions, and to think outside the box—all the more so in business, where everything is quantifiable and measured financially. Beyond self-confidence, it seemed to me, dreams weren't made just by grit, but required some good luck. Early in 1986, some came my way.

Suliman Olayan made it a habit each morning to call or meet with staff on his team. At his office in London one day, after I finished my briefing, he asked me if there was anything else I wanted to discuss.

Yes, "Coca-Cola," I said.

"Go on."

"I think we should look into the possibility of helping Coca-Cola restart operations in the Arab World. Take a chance on entering the Saudi market."

Coca-Cola had been on the Arab boycott list for twenty-five years. It seemed to me that they were exactly the type of partner we needed.

"Do you have any idea what the obstacles are?" he asked.

"The US government, the Arab League, boycott offices in Cairo and Damascus, Israel and many Arab government officials," I answered. "Did I leave anyone out?"

"I'm not optimistic about your chances," he said. "But discuss it with your colleagues. I'll see how I can help."

I knew this wouldn't be simple. The Coca-Cola Company's history in the Middle East was entangled with the Israeli-Palestinian conflict. Being perhaps the most recognizable brand in the world at the time made it a political football and an easy target for each side to use to score political points.

Since 1948, but especially after the 1967 war, when the Arab League became more involved, companies with business interests and investments in Israel were placed on a boycott list. Those actions didn't go without retaliation from the US government. In 1976, President Jimmy Carter signed legislation forbidding US companies from complying with the Arab Boycott and its rules, or even communicating with the Boycott offices. This made it even harder to assist boycotted US companies.

Months after this conversation, good news came in the summer of 1986 when I learned that Suliman, with the help of one of Coca-Cola's board members, had arranged for us to meet in London with the Coca-Cola international team, headed by Claus Halle, its president.

Unfortunately, the meeting didn't bear much fruit. The Coca-Cola team expressed concern and sensitivity about a return to the Arab region. They clearly did not want to violate US laws or harm their business in the States. We were all disappointed, especially me since I was pinning a great deal of hope on adding this iconic company to our portfolio. But we were left with a hint of hope when Claus Halle suggested that I maintain contact with Geoff Unsworth, Middle East director, to find a way to get them out of this jam.

As difficulties unfolded I grew discouraged, but couldn't give up. I felt certain that Coca-Cola had a future in the Arab world, and that our group would be a part of it.

Then in the fall of 1986, after months of hard work, a breakthrough happened. Eager to find a place on the world stage, Saudi Arabia announced it would host a major international soccer tournament—FIFA's Youth World Cup—between February 16 and March 3, 1989. Coca-Cola enjoyed an exclusive worldwide sponsorship agreement with FIFA. The agreement stipulated their product's presence in every one of the FIFA tournaments, and each host nation was expected to comply.

Saudi Arabia was intent on seeing the tournament proceed as scheduled. The Minister of Youth and Sports, the late Prince Faisal Bin Fahd Bin Abdul Aziz, urged on by FIFA, agreed to grant permission for Coca-Cola products to be sold, only in tournament venues and solely for the duration of the tournament. This was a major win for our efforts, and also a good spearhead for future business. So it was important to formalize the relationship, first in a letter of understanding, and later in a joint-venture Saudi company.

Delivering all the products to the country in time for the tournament became a logistics nightmare. But bolstered by our progress, I viewed it as a welcome challenge. Coca-Cola did finally succeed in vending again in the region, at all the tournament games, for the first time after an absence of twenty-five years. I felt momentary relief as I watched Saudi soccer fans lining up to reach for one of those magical red cans.

The first battle had been won. But the mission of permanent return was not yet accomplished. I realized it would still be an uphill challenge.

After much effort, we found a Saudi partner who proved very effective. He helped get a decree issued on August 14, 1988, by the Kingdom's Council of Ministers to drop the court case against the company and remove Coca-Cola from the boycott. This was tantamount to giving a green light to find a bottler, and by 1989 we had begun to get organized to build our own bottling plants. This led me to search for growth opportunities in the region—especially in Palestine. Such a venture could create business and employment opportunities for Palestinians in the occupied territories of the West Bank and Gaza. And someday, it would.

Closing this deal with Coca-Cola and overcoming the boycott tested my negotiation skills and boosted my self-confidence in dealing with multinationals and the global corporate world. But the best reward was a gift from my cartoonist friend Mahmoud Kahil, a cartoon depicting a coke bottle jumping over the boycott fence.

The good work done on the Saudi venture strengthened the relationship between Coca-Cola and the Olayan Group. Coca-Cola looked at us as a credible, compatible strategic partner. Frequently, Saudis faced implicit prejudice in the business world. They were thought to have lucked into "dumb money," wealth they didn't really deserve. I made every effort to counter this stereotype and to dispel misconceptions, especially about the Olayan Group.

In 1998, the relationship between Coca-Cola and the Olayan Group took another positive turn at the World Economic Forum, when I met with Douglas Ivestor, the new chairman of Coca-Cola. He and I had developed a good friendship over the years. At breakfast, he introduced me to Neville Isdell—someone I knew well—as the chairman and CEO of the new Coca-Cola Beverages company. Ivestor discussed expansion plans and the need for a strategic partner to help with further mergers and acquisitions to make Europe the largest Anchor bottler. He asked if the Olayan Group would be interested.

I spoke with Suliman Olayan and with Aziz Syriani, the president, recommending that we proceed. Suliman agreed, in principle. Ivestor and Neville were delighted. In the end, we gained about twelve and a half percent, worth close to two hundred million dollars, and a seat on the board. I was thrilled to be asked to serve on the board.

A year later, we resumed efforts to merge Coca-Cola Bottling with Hellenic, the Greek bottler headed by Andrew David, an exceptionally smart executive. Neville Isdell closed the deal, in which Hellenic acquired Coca-Cola Bottling to form Coca-Cola Hellenic Bottling. The Olayan Group completed a share exchange and I kept a seat on the board and audit committee, serving on both for about ten years. The company today is one of the largest Coke bottlers and operates in more than thirty countries in Europe and Nigeria. After fifteen years, the company is still going strong.

On September 13, 1993, the Oslo Accords were signed. Optimism grew about the possibility of new beginnings for Palestinian businesses in the West Bank and Gaza. This was a good time to pursue further my interest in the bottling business for Palestine, which I conveyed to Coca-Cola chairman Doug Daft and his team. He promised to look favorably at my request and to let me know, once the political situation had settled down.

I knew that for this to materialize, I needed help. I talked to two colleagues—Zahi Khouri, who returned to Ramallah under the Oslo Accords, and Akram Hijazi, a good friend—and convinced them to join the venture. At the same time, I decided to brief Suliman Olayan and request his approval.

Suliman agreed to our involvement, as he firmly believed that Palestinian businessmen have the responsibility to create employment opportunities for Palestinians. Zahi took a lead role after both Akram and I were unable to join because of lack of funds.

Despite all sorts of havoc created by the Israeli bottler, this finally succeeded. The Palestinian Bottling Company was granted the bottling rights for the West Bank, and later for Gaza. Zahi, with a group of Palestinian businessmen, and Coca-Cola were invited to join as partners.

Some twenty years later, in 2014, the Coca-Cola Company press center described the results of this venture and their commitment to it.

Today, Coca-Cola employs 400 associates across three Palestinian bottling plants in Ramallah, Jericho and Tulkarem and seven distribution centers, and our business supports a further 4,000 Palestinian households through retail and across our supply-chain. We are proud to be the country's third largest employer and fifth largest investor.

...We are also proud to have been involved in dozens of community initiatives over the last 16 years [10]

During my visit to Israel, in the summer of 2016, Abla and I had the chance to stop in Ramallah and tour the Palestine Bottling Company offices and plant. I was pleased to see the results of this investment: the bottling plants, the jobs created, the many Palestinian households supported through retail. As a Palestinian, the success of this venture made me proud. It was heartening to see firsthand the venture's ripple effects on our economy and society.

Professionally, my work was satisfying and life affirming. But even as I entered my sixties, my conscience as a Palestinian always reminded me of my identity. I felt a persistent sense of guilt that I wasn't doing enough to alleviate the type of suffering and humiliation that my parents and family experienced after losing their home and identity, and that was continuing with new generations.

An article about the success of a Romanian Jewish refugee in regaining her family home, which appeared in the *International Herald Tribune,* in December of 2000 caught my attention. The article sparked hope that I could achieve similar results for my parents before they died. Written by David Binder, it was entitled "Romanian-Born Jew Wins Battle for her Villa."

Jacqueline Waldman announced with a face full of smiles that she got her house... built 62 years ago in Romania. The villa was confiscated in 1940 under anti-Semitic laws and remained ever after in government hands. Mrs. Waldman, a US citizen who was born in Romania, learned about the long-lost villa from relatives after the fall of communism in 1989. She has pressed a suit as a sole surviving heir to recover the property. After a long journey in the Romanian courts, the Supreme Court of Romania decreed that she could claim possession of the home.

This report affected me strongly. Was my situation as a Palestinian refugee so different from Mrs. Waldman's?

Earlier that year, prior to reading the article, I had visited Jaffa, hoping to see my ancestral home and place of birth. The current resident in the house, a Russian Jew who came to Israel under the 1973 "birthright" law, refused my request to see the house, which he said was given to him by the Israeli government. He loudly refused my wife's plea to allow me a brief look inside, just to refresh my memories.

Of course, I didn't get my ancestral home back. Yet, after all that has happened in the past sixteen years to Palestinians and Jews, including the assassination of Mr. Yitzhak Rabin, I see more people changing, turning away from closed minds on both sides.

After reading Jacqueline Waldman's story, I became interested in finding out more about the history of that time period and why this happened to her family and other Jews there. So, on a business trip to Poland, I decided to take advantage of my time there to expand my knowledge and understanding of that era.

I had joined a team from Coca-Cola Hellenic to meet the Coke management team in Poland. When we arrived at the Warsaw airport, it was freezing cold. A bus took us to La Regina Hotel, where we enjoyed dinner and stayed the night. We were scheduled to visit the Coca-Cola plant at Radzymin. On the way from the airport, I sat next to a good friend from Turkey. We both noticed the roadside signs alongside the highway saying "Krakow."

"This would be a chance to understand more about the history of the period." I said to my friend. "Let's drop what's scheduled for tomorrow and go see the camp." He agreed.

We skipped the tour of the Tylicz water plant the next morning, traveling instead with a driver/guide in a car from the Sheraton Krakow. The guide drove us through a heavy blizzard until, not far from Krakow, we approached the area where the camp had been located. We saw little but sparsely wooded hills and fields. As we got closer, we could hear an eerie silence, interrupted by the sound of blowing snow. At the main entrance to the camp was a sign.

Dear Visitors
    You Are Entering The Site Of The Former
Concentration Camp Plaszow.
Please Respect The Grievous History Of The Site.

Our guide explained that the camp was intended as a forced labor camp and populated with prisoners captured during the liquidation of the Krakow ghetto, which took place from March 13 to 16, 1943. I was particularly shocked to realize that the railroad tracks were laid for only one purpose, the death of innocent people.

What I'd seen in the camp left me to wonder how human beings could inflict such atrocities on others, or that anyone should be forced to endure such a camp. I left Plaszow deeply distraught.

On my way back, I thought about the intertwined histories of the two peoples—Jewish and Palestinian. Does one suffering justify another? The Holocaust, the Nakba, unending decades of military occupation and expulsion of Palestinians from our homelands—how do we help write new histories, ones that offer hope?

Perhaps we help write them by recognizing and learning from all those working bravely each day in countless small ways to overcome mistrust, intolerance and hatred. By learning to stand together, so that this cycle of cruelty and injustice can be broken.

AUB board of trustees at Marquand House, June 1970.
I am in the second standing row, second from right.

Our last Palm Sunday in Beirut, 1975. Left to right: Ramez, me, Ziad and Abla.

Abla's graduation from Richmond University, London 1997.
Left to right: Ziad, me, Abla, and Ramez.

Ziad and Ramez at Ramez's wedding,
July 2001, in London.

The 50th anniversary of the Olayan Group.
Left to right: Abddullah al-Mouallimi, Akram Hijazi, Lubna Olayan,
Neville Isdell, me, Aziz Syriani, and Khalid Olayan.

A cartoon depiction of the return of
Coca-Cola to the Arab world
by Mahmoud Kahil.

Suliman Olayan

With my cohorts in the Advanced Leadership Initiative at Harvard, 2009.
Left to right, first row: Hansueli Maerki, Dr.Charles Denham, Dr. Donald Arthur,
Kenneth Colburn; second row: Jamie Kaplan, Vivian Derryck, Dr. Pablo Pulido;
third row: Paul Addis, Shelly London, me, Hope Woodhouse, Susan Leal and Robert
Whelan. Missing: Astronaut and former head of NASA, Charles Bolden.

My Olayan Group colleague, Khaled
Akhrass (right) and me in front of our
office in London, 1986.

III

17
SERVING OTHERS

I began my career working for universities and nonprofits—AUB, the University of California, Ford Foundation—where the idea of service is at the heart of things. I moved to the corporate world to be able to provide financial security and educational opportunities for my family. Even in the corporate world, the idea of service was always important to me. It was like some kind of watchdog that kept making me ask myself what was I really accomplishing?

Over the years I was in the business world, the idea of corporate social responsibility came into currency. Its advocates argued that companies have a responsibility to all the people whose lives they affect. A company's honesty, integrity, respect for others, and contributions to the well-being of the community all needed to be taken seriously—voluntarily—as measures of success. Too often the term became a catchword, window dressing covering up business as usual. At the same time, the idea was a sign of much needed change that made a real impression on me. Coca-Cola was one corporation I got to know that seemed to take these ideas seriously. But in fact, my earliest real introduction to social responsibility was the sacrifices my family made and the thoughtful generosity of strangers who helped us along the way.

~

In June 2001, I received an unexpected phone call from the director of development and external affairs at the Harvard Kennedy School of Government. The call was an invitation from the school's dean, David Ellwood, to join his advisory board. The Kennedy School was created for students inspired by JFK's call to service. It attracts people who want to work in government, public agencies and nonprofit organizations. Before accepting the appointment, when I met with Dean Ellwood, he told me he wanted to expand the school's mission to benefit more people from the Middle East by improving public leadership and policies.

This opportunity seemed like a godsend, a chance to help extend the spirit of the call for service in the Middle East. My hope was to win funding and support to train public servants who could help build up the region. The first US-Iraq War made it clear to me that the US sorely needed to deepen its understanding of countries in the Arab world. I could imagine no better place than the JFK School to help accomplish that. In a serious effort to support this initiative, the dean hired a former US diplomat, Barbara Bodine, who had extensive knowledge of the region, to spearhead the Middle East program. She organized workshops and seminars, and brought some fellows to assist in the endeavor. She and a group of us from the Dean's Advisory Council were to help in the effort. Resistance from some faculty circles and funding were a challenge at the start. But I'm heartened to see that today the initiative is still active and successful.

As a member of the advisory council, I contacted business and government leaders in the Arab World to try to persuade them to finance a JFK program, specially tailored to regional needs. My idealistic hopes and expectations were tempered by hard facts. Philanthropy is not well established in the Middle East. When it comes to sharing wealth, the pattern of loyalty remains the same as in the past. First comes self, next comes close family, then distant relations, and then finally clan—in that order. The culture is changing, but slowly.

I served on the JFK advisory council until 2009, and while the results of our efforts during that time were mixed, the appointment would open the door for more chances to work in education.

In 2002 an opportunity came, to serve on the board of trustees of the Thunderbird School of Global Management, which I did for ten years. Since its inception in 1946, the Thunderbird School has trained business students from around the world. The school was established on a World War II airbase in Glendale, Arizona, by General Barton Kyle Yount, who obtained the airfield for the express purpose of developing a school focused on international trade and global relations. The school's vision was coined by an original faculty member: *"Borders frequented by trade seldom need soldiers."* The school's mission is, *"To educate global leaders who create sustainable prosperity worldwide."*

One of my projects for Thunderbird was to help introduce the program to Saudi government officials at Saudi Arabia General Investment Authority. My task was to arrange for a team of trustees to be invited to Riyadh to discuss how the school could help in training programs for civil service employees. This meeting led to a substantial contract over several years for Thunderbird to offer courses to executives from government agencies, including Saudi Arabian Basic Industries Company.

Like many educational institutions after September 11, Thunderbird suffered from a decline in international students. At Thunderbird, forty percent of the student body were foreign students. US Immigration was strict in issuing student visas, so the school lost a big source of income. As a result, the school continued to struggle financially until 2014, when the board decided to become a unit of Arizona State University, which has enabled it to continue to successfully operate with autonomous status.

~

While vacationing in Deer Valley, Utah, luck alone helped Abla and I meet Deedee Corradini and her husband John. What attracted us most to her, beyond her charming personality, were the stories we heard about her connection to the Arab world, her passion for and love of Lebanon. On top of that, the fact that she spoke Arabic doubled our interest.

Deedee was born in Providence, Rhode Island. Her minister father moved their family to Beirut in 1955 where he assumed the position of president of the Near East School of Theology, and would later become president of Aleppo College in Syria. From age four to fifteen, Deedee and her family lived in Beirut. As a teenager in the 1960s, she enjoyed Beirut and made close friendships. Like the children of most expatriate families, she was enrolled at the American Community School.

Both the American Community School and International College in Beirut encourage students to think freely, to be inquisitive and to respect the opinions of others. They welcome students from different ethnic backgrounds, religions, social statuses and political affiliations, and they encourage these students to get to know and learn from one another.

In befriending us, Deedee made sure to include us in her busy social program. Her long career in politics was crowned by her election for two terms as mayor of Salt Lake City from 1992 to 2000—a first by a woman, a Democrat and non-Mormon.

Deedee also served on the board of trustees of her alma mater, the American Community School, and persuaded me to join the board, on which I served with pride until 2016. This connection, thanks to Deedee, made it possible to return to Beirut with Abla, and to where I grew up. The trustees of the American Community School gave us a genuinely warm welcome, an emotional experience that felt like a true homecoming.

Another board of trustees on which I was honored to serve, on behalf of the Olayan Group, was American Near East Refugee Aid. ANERA is a highly respected aid organization, active since the 1960s. Over the years, it has steadily assisted Palestinian refugees in Jordan, Lebanon, the West Bank and Gaza, opening schools and providing job training, healthcare and other services.

Palestinians in Gaza are dependent on outside resources, and ANERA has helped Gazans with critical support, especially while the area remains under blockade or during Israeli military attacks. It has staffed medical facilities and provided supplies and other essentials on a continuous basis.

Among ANERA's unique programs that impressed me most was an initiative started by Fawzi Kawash to help overcome low primary school attendance by distributing milk and cookies to children in Gaza. It may sound trivial, but not to those receiving the milk and cookies. The program motivated children to go to school, despite their fears of Israeli soldiers and tanks. Milk and cookies were the incentive.

~

During my time at the Kennedy School, participating in a think tank on education, I met Bill Kruvant and his wife, Charito Kruvant, partners at Creative Learning of Washington D.C. This educational consulting firm has worked for the US government on many contracts in the developing world.

Through Bill and Charito, I was introduced to Ben Orbach, who had spent ten years as a State Department official. Ben wrote *Live from Jordan: Letters Home from My Journey through the Middle East* and worked to build partnerships between the United States and the Muslim world.

Ben and I coauthored an article entitled "The Mubarak Moment: An Opportunity for Israelis," just as the Egyptian uprising was starting.[11] In January 2011, Egyptians took to the streets to try to change the political status quo. It seemed to us both that this might be an historic moment for Israel to break the Arab-Israeli deadlock. The article urged Israelis to extend an olive branch of support to a popular, democratic movement.

Bill Kruvant and Ben Orbach developed the concept of America's Unofficial Ambassadors, on whose advisory board I served from its inception in 2010 until 2016. This initiative catalyzed a movement of American volunteers—college students, community leaders, diplomats and ordinary citizens—to serve on a short-term basis in the Muslim world in fields such as education, health and civic participation. I was attracted by their vision, which was to improve America's relationship with the Muslim world through person-to-person communication and exchange. This was done in classrooms, welfare organizations and civil society settings. Among the success stories were ones coming out of Indonesia, Malaysia and Egypt.

The enthusiasm of young Americans going out and serving gave me hope and confidence. Social responsibility seems to be part of who we are as people. Even if it gets covered over by anger or discouragement, it's still there, waiting. This belief underlies my optimism that what is fair and just will eventually prevail.

18
LOOKING FORWARD

While working for the Olayan Group, I attended the World Economic Forum as a company representative. Held annually in Davos, in the Swiss Alps, the forum's stated aim is to encourage public-private cooperation and entrepreneurship in the public interest by bringing together leaders from government, business, international organizations, education and the nonprofit sector.

Critics characterize the forum as a meeting of elites who are responsible for many of the wrongs in this world. They view it as an event where the exercise of global power and privilege is negotiated and wealth inequality is deepened. Attending this event over the years, it became clear that powerful political, corporate and government leaders do play the key role at Davos, but not only in negative ways.

Davos is also attended by leaders of universities and trade unions, by human rights advocates, artists and others, who gather to share ideas, meet new people, and hear from experts on a wide variety of topics and promote initiative. Participants give lectures, participate in joint panels and listen to one another.

Proceedings remain confidential, which encourages attendees to speak openly and candidly about their interests and concerns. F. W. de Klerk and Nelson Mandela met at Davos for the first time outside South Africa. Davos would never be complete without the presence of grassroots advocates challenging globalization, environmental degradation, capitalistic greed, and gender inequality.

The Olayan Group regularly sent representatives to Davos. Depending on their availability, Khalid Olayan and his sisters attended over the years. Khalid, as chairman, was well known in business circles there, and Lubna and Hutham, two Saudi women running one of the world's largest multinational family-owned groups, received much attention. With their intelligence, acumen and successful track record in business, they shattered stereotypes of Saudi and Arab women, and gained the respect of their peers on an international platform.

Lubna, for example, was the first woman in Saudi Arabia to deliver a keynote address at the Jeddah World Economic Forum. Broadcast live on television, it had the support and encouragement of the late King Abdullah, of Saudi Arabia. I worked closely with Lubna during my tenure with the group. In those annual WEF meetings, she and I arranged many senior-level meetings with business partners and associates to discuss the state of our joint ventures, while at the same time looking for new opportunities to grow and expand the enterprise with new partners.

Since 1996, Abla and I attended Davos together, very much as a team. In her unique, understated way, Abla "worked the room" as much as I did. Her introduction to the wife of Dr. James Farris, an executive and director of CH2M, an American engineering firm, eventually led to a joint venture between CH2M and the Olayan Group. And her gentle but insistent reminders that we take advantage of the social and cultural nooks and crannies of Davos paid off in ways I would not have anticipated.

Globalization has always been an intense topic at Davos, with many praising its promise of myriad benefits to the world economy. I observed all of this from a different perspective. My job with the Olayan Group had given me a chance since the early 1990s to visit many of our US manufacturing partners, in places like Racine and Neenah, Wisconsin; Akron and Columbus, Ohio; and other such cities. I saw firsthand how globalization destroyed the lives of many families and individuals who depended on those manufacturing jobs. The depressed rust-belt communities helped me understand why many clamored to raise their voices in protest at Davos.

Globalization encouraged and enabled manufacturing operations to look for locations around the world to lower labor costs. Many companies relocated and left behind disgruntled and increasingly desperate workers who felt neglected by their employers and political representatives. Though some were treated fairly financially, the other issue was the loss of pride, and feeling of belonging to a worthy enterprise. Over time, this loss cost workers and their families dearly, but adding injury to insult was the loss of earning power that accompanied the end of well-compensated union jobs. In retrospect, globalization benefited greedy managers and bankers much more than the average worker.

The Israeli-Palestinian conflict traveled around the world, from Camp David to Oslo to Madrid, and it touched down twice in Davos in fairly dramatic fashion. In 1994, Arafat and Peres shook hands for the first time there. Then in 2001, Abla and I attended a wonderful dinner for some twenty people, including a gracious Yasser Arafat. Dinner guests looked forward to the general session scheduled for the next day, when Shimon Peres and Arafat would announce the agreement their delegations had reached at a meeting in Taba, Egypt.

Peres and Arafat walked into the session holding hands and smiling. Arafat was scheduled to speak first, but he deferred to Peres. The session was broadcast live, with Kofi Annan, UN Secretary General, sitting in the front row. After Peres spoke positively of the meeting in Egypt, Arafat spoke. He launched into a scathing denunciation of the Israelis and Israel, and didn't say a word about the agreement they had reached. Many forum participants felt that the session was the biggest missed opportunity for the two sides.

The reason for this shift from Arafat was a topic of intense debate among different people both in and outside the Forum. I believed that the cause was pressure from Palestinian groups and Arab countries opposed to the Oslo Accords from the start, who saw them as capitulation to Israeli demands. Arafat may have thought that he could appease his opponents and find a new opportunity where he could bargain for more. But that moment never came.

That same day, Abla and I attended a regional forum on terrorism featuring panelists such as US Homeland Secretary Michael Chertoff, Israeli minister of foreign affair Tzipi Livni and the Arab League Secretary-General Amr Moussa. It was moderated by *New York Times* columnist Thomas Friedman.

Ms. Livni spoke only of Palestinian terrorists, especially suicide bombers. When the moderator opened the session to questions from the audience, the moderator recognized Abla to speak. Abla said that when we speak of terrorism, we can't just pick and choose what suits us. We need to look at the whole picture, including Zionist terrorists, too. Abla's comment made Livni furious. She interrupted Abla and would not let her ask her question.

Afterward, people asked Abla about Livni's outburst. Abla speculated that Livni wanted to avoid any mention of her father, who was a commander of Irgun, the organization responsible for the 1946 bombing of the King David Hotel.

~

Abla insisted that I attend sessions on topics other than business and politics, such as one offering described by Nico Daswani of the Forum staff.

> To complement the important conversations and debates on global challenges, we have created something akin to a set of artistic interventions—performances, screenings, visual displays and immersive installations—in an effort to make those global challenges personal and to inspire our community of leaders to see hope even where the circumstances are bleak.

We met the great violinist and conductor Yehudi Menuhin, and visual artist Dale Chihuly, who created amazing glass sculptures. We met writers such as Paulo Coelho, the Brazilian author of *The Alchemist*, and Frederic Brenner, the French photographer who documented Jewish communities around the world. We attended sessions on scientific topics and met James Watson, discoverer of the DNA double helix structure, and Oliver Sacks, the neurologist and author who wrote *Awakenings* and *The Man Who Mistook His Wife for a Hat*. We heard the clinical psychologist Kay Redfield Jameson discuss her personal experiences with, and research on, bipolar disorder. Frank Sulloway, another psychologist, talked about birth order and its effect on personality, and developmental psychologist Howard Gardner spoke on multiple intelligences. These sessions helped a numbers person like me better understand how the arts and sciences could contribute to the thinking processes of businesspeople.

Paulo Coelho's writings connect common human experiences and questions, addressing themes of love, religion, and morality. Frederic Brenner's photos document Jewish immigrants in the global diaspora, and their attempt to meld old traditions with new environments. Oliver Sacks draws on his experience with patients and his neurological knowledge of the functioning of the brain—"the most incredible thing in the universe"—to create stories that open our thinking.

At Davos, I joined several panels on topics dealing with the Middle East. One was a post-US occupation panel that discussed building and reconstruction for Iraq immediately after the war. The panel considered different business opportunities, which could benefit the Iraqi, Arab and global economies. Unfortunately, nothing really happened and the situation went from bad to worse. Operation Iraqi Freedom ended up opening the way for sectarian, ethnic and religious wars in the region. If this had been the desired outcome of those who waged the war, it would have been fair to celebrate a mission accomplished.

Dr. Klaus Schwab, founder of the WEF's predecessor, the European Management Forum, in his effort to encourage a regional focus, selected several members, including myself, to form a team to start work on establishing a Middle East North

Africa regional forum. The MENA Forum is a WEF regional conference that focuses on issues pertinent to the region: education, refugees, health. On several occasions the Forum came up with initiatives to help solve intricate challenges. The first meeting was hosted in Egypt, followed by Jordan. Those regional meetings were successful and continue to happen every year.

~

At the Forum in 2007, Abla and I attended a session on global demography and aging led by Dr. David Bloom, a professor of economics and demography in the Department of Global Health and Population at the Harvard School of Public Health. Bloom's research focuses on demography, education and labor.

Bloom noted that as life spans increase, a talent pool of highly skilled elders is growing. How might this resource be tapped to contribute to society in productive ways?

At lunch with David Bloom, Abla asked him, "How might someone like Samir utilize his knowledge and experience now?" David said that work he was doing with several Harvard colleagues, led by Rosabeth Moss Kanter, a sociologist and faculty member at the Harvard School of Business, might offer some possibilities, and he promised to stay in contact.

A little more than a year later, David sent us information about the Advanced Leadership Initiative (ALI) at Harvard, which he co-chaired. The group was composed of distinguished Harvard faculty from several disciplines. He asked if I would be interested in participating.

The timing was ideal. I was finalizing retirement plans with the Olayan Group and was eager to start out on a new path. And Abla and I looked forward to being closer to our sons and grandchildren in California. At that time both Ramez and Ziad were already settled in Los Angeles, Ramez and his wife Ambereen with their children, Ziad starting his career in the entertainment industry.

Karla McGuire Minar, the Harvard program coordinator, wrote and officially invited me to join the Initiative as a Harvard Fellow. In a follow-up phone call, Karla offered some insights into the program.

"This new third stage in higher education will prepare experienced leaders to take on new challenges in society, where, potentially, they can make a greater impact than they did in their careers," Karla Minar explained.

Before committing to the program, I traveled to Cambridge in the summer of 2008 to meet and talk with faculty members. I was introduced to Karla, to Rosabeth Kanter and to her co-chair, Fernando Reimers, from the Harvard School of Education, as well as to Nitin Nohria and Rakesh Khurana from the Harvard Business School. The visit gave me an opportunity to learn more about the program's purpose and mission.

Rosabeth Kanter described the initiative as "a collaboration of Harvard faculty members on an academic innovation that has the potential to become another facet, a third stage, of higher education." Fellows would tackle challenging subjects such as poverty, global health, the environment and basic education. "These Fellows excelled in business, and they can do great things for society at large," she said. Here was a real opportunity to make a difference in the lives of people by participating in a program at a university blessed with unique resources.

After receiving a note from Rosabeth welcoming me to the program, in the fall of 2008 I received a formal letter informing me of my appointment as an Advanced Leadership Initiative Fellow. Abla received a letter informing her that she had been accepted as an Advanced Leadership Initiative Partner. I phoned Abla from Cambridge, and we shared our excitement.

Not long after, there would be more cause for celebration. During the first days of our orientation week at the ALI program, we received news that our granddaughter, Ranya, had arrived safely. She would be our third grandchild, along with our other granddaughter, Yasmine, and our grandson, Leyth.

~

Right from the start, the group Fellows at ALI got along well. I immersed myself in the intellectual life of the university with curiosity and a hunger to learn. I realized how much I had missed academia and the world of education. The staff assured us that we would have opportunities to meet with undergraduates, graduate students and faculty. Over the first few weeks, we attended think tanks, seminars and lectures.

I was interested in how to provide expertise and resources for building progressive education in developing nations, especially to help unleash the minds of students in the Arab world. I spoke with Professor Fernando Reimers, director of graduate studies in the School of Education. He firmly believed that any school reform must begin at the earliest stages of education. I attended his lectures and spoke with faculty knowledgeable about the Middle East. I learned that for educational systems in the region to bloom, school principals needed training to help train their teachers. Reimers introduced me to several graduate students who would work on my project. We called it "training the trainers" and presented it at the end of my first-year fellowship to ALI faculty, cohorts and guests as a future road map.

I loved interacting with these bright young people who were full of energy and ready to conquer the world. They seemed to enjoy the chance to interact with a man the age of their parents who had made his career in the world of international business. This was in 2009, a year into the financial crash. I was witness to the dissatisfaction disillusionment of Harvard students—how fed up they were with the greed of businessmen. Many stopped looking for jobs with companies like Goldman Sachs and started looking for positions in non-profit organizations, or in the public sector. They made me proud, and I felt honored to work with them.

Another project I had the pleasure to support was led by Paul Beran, director of the Harvard Outreach Center at the Center for Middle East Studies, who asked me to collaborate with him to grow his Teacher Leadership Program in the Middle East. This new program focused on training American and Middle Eastern K–12 teachers to take leadership roles in introducing into their curriculum topics emphasizing the Middle East region and the United States, including the relationship between the West and Islam.

The program had three components: onsite learning at Harvard, in-region learning, and the application of learning in classrooms. Beran hoped to expand on a successful forum that had been tested in Egypt by adding communication technology to in-region partnerships with schools and organizations in Turkey, Jordan and the wider Middle East Gulf region.

With the election of Barack Obama in 2008, the teacher project generated optimism. Obama spoke of his interest in building bridges with Arabs and with Islam. In Ankara, Turkey, on April 6, 2009, he said, "I know that the trust that binds us has been strained, and I know that strain is shared in many places where the Muslim faith is practiced." At Cairo University two months later, Obama spoke again of reconciliation and bridge building, offering his vision of a resolution to the Palestinian-Israeli conflict. Obama's sentiments, rarely uttered in Washington, were well received by Egyptians and others in the Arab world, and they inspired our work at Harvard.

Unfortunately, this positive beginning, though welcomed among Arab peoples, didn't last long. Looking back at events, I realize that there were many centers of power, including local, regional and global players, who worked hard to thwart Obama's initiative, each for their own narrow agenda.

Some saw Obama's efforts as a threat. His encouragement of free thinking, an open civil society and political dialogue could lead to a loss in power. Others in the region considered his opening a threat in the struggle for regional dominance. Israel saw closer ties between America and the Arab World as potentially weakening their strategic partnership with the US.

All of this occurred at a time when Islamic radicals were carrying out terrorist attacks in Europe and the Middle East, which infuriated the general public and successfully tarnished, through media and political narratives, the reputation of Islam and all Muslims, including several million American citizens.

Despite all this, Paul Beran and I were determined to proceed with teacher leadership work in the Middle East. We both tried, through my business connections, to raise funds and find sponsors from companies that had a long and rewarding presence in the region. Unlike the corporate world, the US Department of Education recognized Beran's work in the Egypt program as an important source of education and training. The education department also awarded Beran's Harvard outreach center a prestigious Fulbright-Hayes project grant to develop a travel-study program for fourteen American K–12 teachers to visit Egypt and Tanzania.

Because of limited funding, the program did not move on—a common story in nonprofit initiatives. But the work we did was encouraging, and it pushed me to keep looking forward.

19
A Pilgrimage

My mother was a person of abiding religious conviction who always affirmed the workings of God in her life. At every cross-road or predicament, she turned to God for help as our savior. Whether it was a school for her children, an apartment for our family or a job for my father, she would tell us, "I prayed this would happen. God made it happen." Every morning she lit a candle before an icon of Santa Teresa. My father was happy to have my mother help him maintain good connections with the ultimate powers that be.

Following my family's experience of being forced from our home in Jaffa, in my early adulthood I became a skeptic. Religion seemed like something for the weak and helpless. I was inspired more by people who were self-reliant. These tended to be people who often had strong doubts about religion—but not necessarily about faith. As a result, so did I. It was a period of time for me when religion and faith seemed to go separate ways. It wasn't until I graduated from college and experienced the unpredictable challenges of the business world, as I witnessed firsthand the suffering of other people whose lives were turned upside down by circumstances beyond their control, that it dawned on me that my mother was right all along. This realization helped me to again find comfort in my religious faith.

I began making Sunday visits to the Greek Orthodox Church near Parliament Square in Beirut. There I could spend time soul-searching and in prayer. By the end of mass, I felt like a heavy burden had been lifted from my shoulders, and I experienced a sense of peace and tranquility. From then on, this renewed faith continued to help and guide me. Whether it was a difficult search for a job after graduation or being involved in the front lines of the business world, it helped steer me.

Another turning point was a group trip to the Burj al Barajneh Palestinian refugee camp in Lebanon that I went on in 2012. The trip was organized by a fellow American Community School trustee. The suffering I witnessed there shocked my system to the core. The camp packed twenty thousand souls into one square kilometer of destitution. Over six decades later, refugees from 1948 were still refugees, as if frozen in time.

Wires hanging in the narrow alleyways exposed the camp's inhabitants to the constant danger of electrocution, which occurred almost monthly. In an emergency, an injured person would be handed from one rooftop to another, until they reached the outside of the camp and an ambulance, because the camp had no real streets. Bodies of the deceased were transported the same way.

While there, I spotted an UNRWA office and remembered how much the agency had been a lifeline for me and my family. In the camp, the need for help was immense, and UNRWA did help, but with limited, precarious funding.

~

Abla had grown up in a family in which the church took a prominent place in their lives. So we made a promise that when we retired, we would go on a pilgrimage to the Holy Land and see how people lived together. A good friend of ours, Zahi Khouri, helped us make plans.

With the beginning of summer 2016, the time for our trip arrived. We flew from Athens to Amman, and from the airport a driver took us to Zahi's house, where our journey was to start.

I was more concerned than Abla about the crossing. I had heard too many stories about long interrogations and hostile security checks. My son had traveled to Israel to attend the wedding of his best friend, a female classmate from college. Even though he was a US citizen, as a Palestinian American he was subjected to a drawn-out interrogation by immigration before he was allowed into the country.

Zahi suggested that we cross from Jordan via the Allenby Bridge, also called the King Hussein Bridge. Bridge crossings are restricted to certain times of day and religious holidays. We arranged to go in the evening. After phoning his contacts, he urged us, "If we leave now, we'll be able to make it to Jerusalem in time." Zahi was born in Jaffa but had become a US citizen. After the Oslo Accords, he returned to Palestine, bought a house in the Old City of Jerusalem and built a business in the West Bank. He crossed the bridge frequently and kept assuring me the crossing would be easy, but I still felt apprehensive.

There are two ways to cross. If you can afford a fee of two hundred dollars per person, you can hire a private security company to help you process the visa and attend to security needs, which can take a few hours. Or, you can stand in a crowd with hundreds of others in punishing heat. Neither Jordan nor Israel offered us any waiver or preference as US citizens. Usually, a car that brings you to the bridge from the Jordanian side of the bridge can't cross because it has Jordanian license plates. Fortunately, our car had Jerusalem license plates, which are perceived as less of a security threat. With a Jerusalem license, you can cross the river both ways with little hassle.

We drove across Allenby Bridge to the Israeli checkpoint. After we crossed the demarcation line, Zahi parked in an area where cars are thoroughly inspected. Then we walked to an old building that serves as a facility to process crossings. The building had two sections, one for the general public and one for people who can afford to pay the two hundred dollars to expedite the process, which we did. We handed over our passports to be checked and then settled in to wait.

An hour later, a pleasant young woman from Israeli security appeared, holding my passport. "Is Samir Toubassy here?" she announced.

I stood up. "Yes, I'm here," I answered.

"Come with me," she instructed.

She looked over my passport.

"Were you born in Palestine?"

"Yes."

"When did you leave Palestine? In1948? 1967?"

"Why do you ask?"

"We keep two sets of security records, for 1948 and 1967," she answered politely.

"1948," I told her.

She continued to barrage me with questions.

"Why are you coming?"

"We are Christians and are on a pilgrimage to Jerusalem, and the Holy sites."

"Do you have any relatives in Ramallah?"

"I do."

"Do you have plans to visit Ramallah?"

"We're not sure."

"Remember that the visa we give you restricts you to the areas under Israeli rule. You cannot visit the occupied territories. What about your wife? Is she a Palestinian?"

"Yes, she was born in Jordan in 1949."

The young woman looked closely again at Abla's passport. "Your wife doesn't look Palestinian," she said, apparently referring to Abla's green eyes and fair skin. "Look at the picture. She looks like one of us, like my grandmother, even."

"How about if you see her in person?" I suggested.

I went to Abla in the lounge. "The security officer thinks you look like them. She wishes to talk to you."

The security officer apologized to Abla. "I didn't mean it that way," she said. But then she quickly resumed asking us questions. Apparently satisfied that we posed no security threat, she told us to go wait in the lounge. An hour later she came back and handed us our passports with a smile. "You can leave now," she said.

As we were getting into the car Zahi told us, "We're done with the difficult part. We'll be in Jerusalem in an hour."

With Zahi's Jerusalem license plates, we were able to pass right through the checkpoints. Driving at night, we gazed at the lights shining on the hills from thousands of homes that are part of settlements erected after the 1967 war, on what was once Palestinian land surrounding the City of Jerusalem. Abla and I were both sadly hypnotized by the scene.

We arrived at the American Colony Hotel in Jerusalem at eleven and checked into our room. Even though it was late, I said to Abla, "Let's go for a walk." I could barely believe that we were in Jerusalem. I wanted to go out and feel the city, breathe the air.

On June 9, 2016, our first day there, we met our guide, Daniel, for breakfast. I told him that, as well as going to holy sites, we wanted to visit with and talk to people, to get a feel for how the two peoples live together.

First, he led us to the Church of the Holy Sepulchre where there were long lines of worshippers waiting to visit the tomb of Jesus. An Armenian priest noticed that Abla was having problems with her knees, so he kindly offered to help.

He informed us, "Our turn to manage the entrance to the tomb is coming soon. Each sect is allotted a specific time to visit the tomb." He added, "You are welcome to join us," which we gladly did. Then he added, "You're Armenian now, okay? Follow me."

After being Armenians for a few minutes, which made it possible for us to see the holy site, we stopped at the area designated for the Armenian Church and lit a candle. With tears in her eyes, Abla thanked the priest for assisting us.

When she was young, during visits to her grandmother, she made daily stops to pray at this sacred place. Being there recharged my faith, reaffirming how important Jerusalem is for Christians. Where would Christianity be without Jerusalem and these holy sites?

We left the church and headed to the Western Wall, also known as the Wailing Wall. Hundreds of Jewish worshippers were heading in the same direction. Many were accompanied by loud klezmer music and appeared to be celebrating bar mitzvahs. As with Islam, Jewish tradition doesn't permit males and females to pray together. Each walked to their separate designated area. To our delight, we heard the noon Call to Prayer from al-Aqsa Mosque, while the bells in the churches rang loudly, sending chills through me. For a moment, I thought that maybe God really did intend for Jerusalem to be a place for all believers to worship peacefully, an example to be followed by the rest of the world.

Two decades after the war of 1948, a second one occurred with similar devastation in the lives of Palestinians. On June 5, 1967, the Israel Defense Forces conquered East Jerusalem, Gaza and the Golan Heights in the Six-Day War. The administration of the holy sites had remained in the hands of Jordan. Sadly, the Israeli victory signaled a new phase in the Palestinian-Israeli conflict, a seemingly never-ending saga of military occupation, checkpoints, searches and restrictions on movement; of house demolitions and land confiscations; limited access to food, water, housing and medical treatment at hospitals or education and employment; of people living under the cloud of possible military assault.

We drove up to view the city from atop the Mount of Olives. From there, the beauty of Jerusalem, surrounded by hills, is plainly visible. Across the way, al-Aqsa Mosque ("the Dome of the Rock"), the Church of the Holy Sepulchre and the Wailing Wall appear nestled together, as if hugging each other.

Our next stop was Bethlehem, where we went to a restaurant situated just outside the wall. This was our first encounter with the separation wall. As we ate our lunch, we observed Palestinian families, women, elderly people, children and laborers, all walking in the scorching heat, carrying heavy bags.

"Buses are not permitted beyond the Israeli checkpoint," Daniel informed us. "Palestinians are dropped off some distance from the wall, then they have to walk to the wall and beyond to their homes." With a stop at a security checkpoint, a few minutes' walk may take more than a half hour.

After lunch, we visited the Church of the Nativity, the traditional site of the birthplace of Jesus. Kneeling in the grotto beneath the church and passing a prayerful hand over the empty center of the silver star with fourteen points embedded in the marble floor, signifying where Jesus was born, left us without words.

From there, we headed to Jericho, to view the Mount of Temptation, where Jesus spent forty days of reflection and was tempted by the Devil. Our last stop for the day was the site on the Jordan River where Jesus was baptized. Both Israel and Jordan claim that the historical site is on their side of the river. There, many people were standing in the water, and Abla joined them. Afterward, she said she felt as if her soul was cleansed.

One of the first things Abla wanted to do while in Jerusalem was to visit her grandmother's house. The house is hundreds of years old and right in the heart of the Old City. To get there, you have to enter the Old City from Damascus Gate, also known as Bab El Amoud Gate, one of the eight gates to the Old City, built by Turkish sultan Suleiman the Magnificent in 1538. Like the other stone portals built inside the historic wall of the Old City, the gates still serve as entry for Palestinians and visitors to sacred and historic places.

As I walked through the narrow alleys, I sensed that every stone I stepped on had withstood the forces of history. Inhabitants inside the city walls are Palestinian. Shops and family businesses have been passed from one generation to the next, despite the many foreign occupiers of the city over the centuries. I was always aware of Israel Defense Forces patrolling the district, their militarized police presence a constant source of discomfort and fear among Palestinian vendors and shoppers.

Prior to 1966, when Abla moved to Berkeley, her family often visited her grandmother on school holidays and summer breaks, and she remembers those times as among the happiest in her early life. She warmly recalls many details about the home: the well inside the house that brought up ice-cold water, the terrace above the second floor and the doors and windows crafted by her carpenter grandfather. Thankfully, unlike Palestinians who had to flee their centuries-old homes, the house is still in the family's hands.

Abla's uncle, an optician in the Old City, remained in the house before and after he married. Abla's cousin took over the optical store after his father's death. On our way to visit the Old City, we stopped in at the shop in Haret al-Nasara, part of the Christian quarter. Walking to the shop along those ancient alleys made me feel why people cling to their homes in a place where the rituals of daily life have persisted for millennia.

Abla's cousin was out, but the staff eagerly wanted to help when Abla introduced herself as his cousin, visiting from the US.

"I would like to see my grandmother's house," Abla told them.

The store assistant phoned her cousin, and within seconds he was on the line. "Yes, I will send the keys to the store. They will be there in half an hour."

When the keys arrived, the assistant walked us to the house. The moment the door opened, it appeared to Abla as if her grandmother's house had been frozen in time. Seemingly, nothing had changed. It was as if the place had been under the hand of an invisible caretaker. Like a little child, Abla stepped inside and into jubilant and lost memories of her family's life.

Abla proudly showed me the house: the staircase banister they used to slide down, her grandmother's favorite place to sit, next to the bay windows where she would watch and wait for peddlers of ka'ak bread rings, baked eggs or falafel.

But on closer inspection, signs of wear and tear became apparent. And the keys to the downstairs bedroom, to the kitchen and to the door leading to the well were all missing. Jerusalem sits atop an aquifer, and for centuries, wells have been dug to access it. Abla wanted badly to see the well, She walked up the stairs and returned with sadness and dismay on her face. Her expression told a different story of the house, its lack of proper care, which resulted from the occupation.

In the Old City of Jerusalem, any change, like repairs to old homes—regardless of how minor—requires special approval from the military authorities. Approval can take forever to grant, or is denied, leaving old Palestinian homes unlivable.

"Well, better a little than nothing at all," Abla said in her endearing, ever-optimistic way.

On Friday morning, we left early to drive to Nazareth, in the Galilee, to visit the Church of the Annunciation, the home of the Blessed Virgin Mary, where the angel Gabriel announced to Mary that she would bear Jesus.

From there we went to Majdal, on the Sea of Galilee, for lunch. Taking in the restaurant's quiet, welcoming atmosphere, we ordered from their menu of familiar Arabic dishes we had eaten all our lives. The food was served with care, and we were warmed by its comforting flavors and presentation. When I asked to meet the chef, he turned out to be a Palestinian Israeli, in his late twenties. He had studied in Europe and worked in two Michelin-rated restaurants before returning. Despite the daily obstacles he and his family faced, food was his way of living and sustaining his heritage.

The region has such a rich cuisine and a long tradition of exquisite food, with Ottoman, Greek, Lebanese, Syrian, Palestinian and Persian roots. As part of a long-standing effort to assert sovereignty over the land and culture, Israel has appropriated food traditions as its own national cuisine, separating them from the diverse Levantine culture within which Arabs in the Middle East prepared these dishes for millennia.

Naturally, cultures borrow from one another. But in the hyper-politicized world of the Palestine-Israel conflict, efforts by Israelis to claim ownership of an historic cuisine, or of other aspects of cultural life, are deeply resented by Palestinians and other Middle Easterners. In an interview, Palestinian actor Salim Dau, who stars in the Israeli political thriller television series *Fauda*, (Chaos),[12] said, "The Jewish Nation-State bill doesn't ruffle me. We have been living this racism for all these years. We feel it everywhere. What angers me most is when Israelis try to own my cuisine."[13]

On Saturday, we headed to Jaffa, where we especially wanted to visit the Arab quarter. Remembering my experience from 2000, when I'd tried to visit my family's home, I had no intention of returning there.

Our driver took us to the harbor area. As we drove slowly through the district, I noticed an old staircase that led to the top of the hill. I urged the driver to stop and go back. "I know those stairs," I told Abla. "My grandmother's house was at the top of that hill. We used to come down those stairs to the beach."

We got out of the car and climbed up the stairs to the main road. There we found old dilapidated houses, one of which I believe was my grandmother's. But the inhabitants of these houses were nowhere to be seen. Strangely, I felt refreshed by even this brief glimpse of what may have been my family's home. But I left with sadness at what was lost.

~

As we were coming down the steps, we spotted an art gallery in a lovely old building overlooking the Mediterranean. With its panoramic view of the sea, the building reflected the Ottoman architectural style typical of the eighteenth-century homes built in Jaffa. The gallery housed the work of a Lithuanian Jewish artist, who had resettled in the city.

The gallery manager showed us some of the artist's work, which had been inspired by the light and colors of the old port of Jaffa. Later, I was introduced to his son. I told him I was Palestinian, born in Jaffa, and asked him if he owned the building.

"No," he said. "It is not possible to own real estate that was confiscated from Palestinians. We can only buy short-term leases from the government. But in recent years the Knesset has made it possible for Jewish citizens to enter into a joint venture ownership with a government agency, which grants the citizen thirty-percent ownership."

Israel is possibly the only country in the free world that owns all real estate in the land without recognizing the rights of its original legal owners.

Visiting Tel Aviv, the financial and fashion capital of Israel, reminded me of stories I'd heard from my mother about her shopping trips there and a time when Palestinians and Jews could live—and shop—together.

In the afternoon, we drove north to Haifa, "the Bride of the Mediterranean," where my mother was born and where my maternal grandfather grew up. Along the way, we passed by Caesarea, the great Roman city that had been a capital in the Roman Empire for more than five centuries.

In the Mount Carmel district of Haifa, we found a restaurant with a lovely, panoramic view of the Mediterranean. After lunch we wanted to visit the Baha'i Temple, which was of special interest to me. My maternal grandfather was a friend of Abdul Baha Abbas, the leader of the Baha'i faith, who passed away on November 28, 1921.

During our lunch, at the next table sat three local women, chatting in Arabic. We introduced ourselves and told them we were Palestinian Americans. The older woman introduced herself and her two daughters.

The mother was born in Haifa. Her parents had never left the city, as did many in Haifa, more than anywhere else in Palestine. Haifa today, she said, was a progressive town where Jews and Arabs coexist in relative harmony. She was in her fifties and a history professor, with friends in Haifa literary and journalist circles. So when I told her about our family's ties to *Al-Nafir* newspaper, she immediately offered to help me locate some missing issues in my collection. She also promised to send me an oral history of Palestine, gathered by faculty from Haifa University.

Her daughters both were college graduates. The younger daughter had just finished school and had applied to several places for employment, but with no luck so far. She admitted that, as a young Palestinian woman, her chances of getting a good job were few. The three of them couldn't hide their dismay about discrimination faced by Arab Israelis in the rest of country. The worst of it was the feeling of being a stranger in their own homeland.

They were keen to talk and learn more about us and our life in the States. Our conversation, comparing notes and questions with this family who had steadily remained in Haifa, warmed our hearts and added a few pieces to the puzzle of our story as a family from the diaspora. Reluctantly, we said goodbye. We needed to get back to the American Colony Hotel to meet friends who had invited us to see Jerusalem by night.

~

Our trip made me feel that a different kind of night has fallen on Jerusalem, a darkness that can be seen in broad daylight. At the King David Hotel, the lobby was filled with affluent guests, mostly from the US. Some were there to celebrate bar mitzvahs. But for me, the King David Hotel was a painful reminder of my Uncle Mitri, killed in the terrorist attack on the British Mandate offices in the hotel by the Irgun, on July 22, 1946. Having lived with this family loss, I was especially disturbed by a plaque at the hotel's entrance. It describes the heinous bombing by a right-wing militant group as "resistance" by underground "freedom fighters." No mention is made of the innocent casualties—British, Palestinians, Jewish and others. Even the names of lost loved ones can be erased with impunity .

Perhaps nothing is more symbolic of this darkness than the wall that Israel began building more than a decade ago. It has become a 425-mile-long hulking concrete barrier, eight meters high, separating Israel from the Palestinian territories and Palestinians from their land, families, schools, healthcare facilities—all in the name of "security." Considered illegal by the United Nations, the wall is a rejection of the norms of the civilized world. More so, it is a challenge to those of us who profess to believe in equality.

The trip made clear to us that things we may take for granted in the US are not necessarily the ethos elsewhere in the world. Driving along the wall on the Israel side and then walking along the Palestinian side made us feel small. This humongous structure overshadows and diminishes people. But our guide shared with us a commonly known secret that, in a ridiculous way, the wall has been good for business, as a new black market is thriving.

Each day, many documented Palestinians legally pass through official checkpoints, to and from work. The wall has spawned a cooperative black market of Israeli and Palestinian smugglers who, for a fee, provide nondocumented Palestinians this daily "service" of accessing employment in Israel. With help from "brokers" on the Palestinian side, workers scale the wall, to be met by brokers on the Israeli side, both sides cooperating—for a fee—to facilitate this risky crossing. If Palestinian and Israeli smugglers can find a way to work together, maybe there's hope that a legalized version of this mutually profitable enterprise might serve as a model for peaceful coexistence by both sides.

On Sunday morning, the driver picked us up at the hotel to head back to Amman. Because of our VIP arrangement, it was easy for Abla and me to cross back into Jordan. But the relative ease of our crossing left me feeling remote from the humiliation and suffering that ordinary Palestinians must put up with. Our pilgrimage reminded me that faith means asking myself, *How might I do more to join with my fellow Palestinians, and others like them, in crossing their separation walls and Allenby bridges?*

20
MY NAKBA

Before I built a wall I'd ask to know
What I was walling in or walling out,
And to whom I was like to give offence.
Something there is that doesn't love a wall,
That wants it down…
—Robert Frost, "Mending Wall"

Not even the most clairvoyant fortune teller could have foretold the consequences of the events that sent my family scurrying for safety in 1948. But the loving support of my parents, their counsel not to give in to self-pity but to work hard in school, as well as my kind and challenging mentors, all helped me try to excel and carried me into adulthood, family and a vocation. As I complete my eighth decade, I realize I have been blessed in countless ways.

At the same time, I have always been trailed by a shadow: the image of a nine-year-old boy, who was rushed with his family from his home in frantic haste, with just a few belongings, to escape a conflict zone. Moving frequently from place to place, without a permanent home, at some point this boy realizes, and finally accepts, that he has lost his family's ancestral homeland, spanning generations, and that things will never be the same again.

I've often wondered what life would have been like if my family hadn't left Jaffa after 1948, if instead we had stayed on the "road not taken," as Robert Frost, my favorite poet from my school days in Beirut, put it. Was my family free to stay or leave? I am not sure. We felt sharply the pressures to leave our homes. Relatives, friends, ordinary people of big cities and small villages felt the push to flee. But my family was also lucky enough to have the wherewithal to get out. At the time, fleeing Jaffa seemed the best choice for the safety of our family. But in retrospect, when I do the math, I doubt that I would make the same decision, despite all I have been able to achieve or the obstacles I would have faced if I had remained.

In a sense, the Nakba forced all Palestinians to become outsiders. In different ways, we were all displaced. We became a new lost tribe, like so many other displaced tribes now trekking across the globe.

~

Our trip to the Holy Land helped me to see that at the heart of the Nakba is *separation*. The expulsion of Palestinians from, or within, our homeland in 1948 separated us—from our homes, our families and loved ones, from our fellow Palestinians; from our cities and villages, land and culture. It separated Palestinians, as a people, from the international community, as a wall of fear was constructed around us in the minds of others—Americans in particular—by making words like "Palestinian," "Muslim" or "Arab" synonymous with evil and terrorism. In different ways, it separated us from ourselves. The separation wall in Jerusalem is surely a fitting symbol of the Nakba. I'm one Palestinian who wants to be told I can return, if only to reclaim my roots, my identity and my sense of self.

The Nakba damaged the fabric of our family. The dispersion of family members left my parents, especially my father, who rarely showed his emotions, distraught. In 1988, deteriorating security finally convinced my parents to leave Beirut, first for Athens where travel papers were secured. There my sister Leila's son met and accompanied them to the Bay Area and a joyous family reunion. They resettled close to Leila and her family. It was only then that being together again allowed me to tally the full price of being separated from them by the fighting in Lebanon. Every time I visited my father, I could see on his wrinkled face the lasting sadness of exile from Jaffa and the scattering of our family.

Yet at times, I could see his love and contentment with what his children had accomplished. When I think of him after all the years since he passed away, those memories fill me with elation and remind me of how fortunate we were to have a father like him. I only regret that I was unable to fulfill his wish to be buried in his church next to his mother in Jaffa, a Palestinian denied the right of return, even in a coffin.

I always struggled to bring a sense of normalcy to my life—getting a good education, finding an amazing partner in Abla, with whom I raised a beautiful family. Our two sons, Ramez and Ziad, from early childhood until they finished college and beyond were independent and responsible, exactly the way Abla and I had hoped. They made careers for themselves and opportunities for their families. Abla and I are now able enjoy more time with them.

As adults, my siblings were scattered to faraway places—Beirut, Amman, Dubai, Paris, Luxembourg, the US—making it difficult for us to gather as a family except on rare occasions. In the last few years, I discovered the whereabouts of, and reconnected with, many of my first cousins with whom I had lost contact. The search extended from Ramallah to Amman, London, Paris, and various cities in the United States. Abla and I have met our cousins' children, all of whom showed a hunger to know more about their heritage.

One American niece of ours, after graduating from college, left a position as a partner in global management consulting to travel to Jerusalem and Ramallah for over a year, volunteering and searching for her roots as the child of a British mother and an Arab Israeli father who became a US citizen. She then enrolled at the School of Oriental and African Studies at the University of London, a program specializing in the study of Asia, Africa and the Middle East. She focused on conflict resolution, hoping one day to contribute to the resolution of the Israeli-Palestinian conflict.

After her return, she said. "Going home was the best feeling I ever had in my life. When I was young, I often wondered why birds fly thousands of miles to return home. I only understood this feeling when my feet touched the ground at Ben Gurion Airport."

Like my niece's journey, my own with this memoir has been one I didn't want to see end. It's been a return that has helped me reconnect with my soul. It gave me a chance to review my life as a child, a teenager, an adult, a husband, a father, a grandfather, as a professional, and as an educator. It gave me the chance to free myself from burdens, inhibitions and mindsets that influenced my life. It's no exaggeration to say that certain moments in writing this story gave me an untold happiness of looking at my life through a new and clear lens. Relationships became vivid, as memories of days both sweet and sour came rushing back with a crisp freshness. All this helped me to re-experience the successes, trials and failures in my race to achieve, and to reconsider the meaning of success.

Throughout my life and career, family, friends, mentors and colleagues and their institutions offered lifelines of respect, generosity and belief in me for which I am indebted. These kinds of ties are the opposite of separation.

Something there is that doesn't love a wall,
That wants it down.

The words of "Mending Wall" remind me of life lessons I cherish most, ones I first learned from my parents and family: hope, ethics, justice, forgiveness, belonging. Perhaps they can help steer us to find ways to bring all of our destructive barriers down. These lessons from home stuck with me when I was young. But even now, at eighty, they inspire and sustain me still.

ENDNOTES

1 Fawaz, Leila Tarazi. (1994). *An Occasion for War: Civil Conflict in Lebanon and Damascus in 1860*. Berkeley: University of California Press.; Farah, Caesar E. (2000). *The Politics of Interventionism in Ottoman Lebanon, 1830–1861*. London: I.B. Tauris. See also "1860 Mount Lebanon civil war." https://en.wikipedia.org/wiki/1860_Mount_Lebanon_civil_war

2 There are many books documenting the history of the depopulation of Palestine that show listing by names, dates, and locations. Readers may find the following books useful references:

   Davis, Rochelle A. (2010). *Palestinian Village Histories: Geography of the Displaced*. Stanford: Stanford University Press.

   Khalidi, Walid. (2006). *All That Remains: The Palestinian Villages Occupied and Depopulated by Israel in 1948*. Washington, DC: Institute for Palestinian Studies.

   Morris, Benny. (2004). *The Birth of the Palestinian Refugee Problem Revisited*. New York: Cambridge University Press.

   See also, iNakkba, a GPS-enabled political web-based app. It allows users to locate Palestinian villages that were destroyed during and after the 1948 war between Jewish forces and local Palestinians and external Arab militaries. It is a tool for learning about the silenced history of this conflict. From this source and others, hundreds of towns and villages could be identified. https://zochrot.org/en/site/nakbaMap

3 http://web.nli.org.il/sites/nlis/en/jrayed/Pages/Al-Nafir.aspx

4 *al-Nafir*, December 2, 1928 issue.

5 See also, *Albert Einstein letter, April 10, 1948, to Mr. Shepard Rifkin*, *i*n response to the later acts depopulating Palestinian villages to make room for Europeans settlers. Albert Einstein refused to meet with visitors associated with fundraising in the US for Zionist paramilitaries. In a letter to Mr. Shepard Rifkin, executive director, American Friends of the Fighters for the Freedom of Israel,

Einstein wrote: *"Dear Sir: When a real and final catastrophe should befall us in Palestine the first responsible for it would be the British and the second responsible for it the Terrorist organizations build up from our own ranks. I am not and will not see anybody associated with those misled criminal people."*

6   Okies were migrant workers from Oklahoma and other areas of the Dustbowl who had been forced to abandon their farms and leave for California during the Depression of the 1930s

7   Siblin Training Center, UNRWA. A training center for twenty-one specializations in Lebanon, for Palestinian refugees' children who finished UNRWA school.

8   Field, Michael. (2000). *From 'Unayzah to Wall Street: The Story of Suliman S. Olayan*. London: John Murray.

9   Sabra and Shatila are two Palestinian refugee camps in Beirut. https://en.wikipedia.org/wiki/Sabra_and_Shatila_massacre

10   The Coca-Cola Company, "Our Coca-Cola Palestinian Business." August 19, 2014. https://www.coca-colacompany.com/press-center/company-statements/our-coca-cola-palestinian-business

11   *Obsidian Wings*. February 2, 2011. https://obsidianwings.blog.com/

12   *Fauda*, Arabic for chaos. An Israeli TV series shown also on Netflix, depicts the two-sided story of the Palestinian-Israeli conflict.

13   *Haaretz*. August 7, 2018, p. 1–6.

Acknowledgments

This book is the work of an amateur writer who spent his life in the business world. It is by no means a history of a region. The art of storytelling, I first learned as a Palestinian youth, is in the telling—not the writing.

Much credit and gratitude go to the many people who helped our family along our road. Without them—people who have enriched our lives, extended a helping hand in difficult times, and mentored us—this journey would never have been possible. To them, I could not be more thankful.

The idea of making this book was hatched in 2009 and 2010 during a fellowship at Harvard University's Advanced Leadership Initiative. I am deeply grateful to Marshall Ganz, of the Harvard Kennedy School, for his workshop on telling your public story, which sparked in me the idea of sharing my life story with a wider audience. At about the same time, miles away in Santa Monica, California, I met Lawrence Owen, formerly of Rasmussen College, whose teaching specialty is writing our personal histories. Larry generously extended a helping hand, building my self-confidence and helping me to edit early drafts of my manuscript.

Along the way, writer Didi Goldenhar provided me with helpful advice on the book's form; Dr. Robert Sauté offered countless hours reviewing and editing early material; Dr. Byron Cannon, professor emeritus of Middle East history at the University of Utah, provided valuable guidance; and James Moran, former European Union diplomat and ambassador, took time to read the manuscript and provide valuable advice. My lifelong friend Dr. Fawwaz Tuqan, professor of Arabic literature and Islamic history at the American University of Beirut, offered steady encouragement; and the talented artist Lauren Dorman, helped develop initial design ideas for the cover.

Serving on committees, boards, and organizations has given me opportunities to listen to others about what they are seeing in the Middle East. These wonderful people, without exception, keep finding reasons for hope. They have helped keep my love for my homeland alive. I am especially thankful to have been given a chance, in a modest way, to advocate for people in a part of the world about whom I care deeply, as they weather the region's calamities, catastrophes and blights.

If I could talk to my parents today, I would thank them for navigating our family through rough, diasporic seas to safe harbors.

Abla, my wife and life partner, has been an immense support and encouragement at all times—especially when I was ready to throw in the towel on the whole project. She dedicated long hours to reading and rereading the manuscript, and providing insightful advice to improve my narrative. Both my children, Ramez and Ziad, though busy with their careers and family responsibilities, took the time to read material and offer constructive comments; my sister Leila Farradj spent hours with me reminiscing about our early years in Jaffa and Lebanon; and my grandchildren inspired, me to write our family story to help them to know who they are now, and always.

My heartfelt thanks to Michel Moushabeck, publisher of Interlink Books, for keeping alive an independent press that provides a platform for voices from around the world; and to Interlink editor John Sobhiea Fiscella, designer Pam Fontes-May, and proofreader Cassie Sanderell for working with me to make my voice heard.

Finally, I thank you—the reader—for accompanying me on this journey.

ABOUT THE AUTHOR

Born in Jaffa in 1939, Samir Toubassy left Palestine with his family in 1948, seeking refuge in Lebanon. He grew up in Beirut, receiving his education at International College and the American University of Beirut. He began his career working in the nonprofit field, first at the Ford Foundation on public administration reform in the Middle East, then at the American University of Beirut, as a director of budget, followed by the University of California after settling in the US, where he received his MBA from Golden Gate University in San Francisco and eventually gained citizenship.

Samir started out in nonprofit management, developing his skills for over a decade. Then he embarked on a new career in the business world, with The Olayan Group, one of the large privately held global business conglomerates, through its Riyadh, Athens, London, and New York offices. Over a period of thirty-five years, he served as president of Olayan Development and as a Group vice president. Having worked closely with the Group's iconic founder, Suliman Olayan, he continued to serve as a senior advisor and member of the Executive Committee until December 2016.

After building a legacy of achievement and contributions in both careers—in the nonprofit and global business worlds—he accepted a two-year senior fellowship at Harvard University to be part of the Advanced Leadership Initiative. This program was designed to prepare experienced professionals take on new challenges, where they potentially can make greater societal impact than they did in their careers.

Samir has served as an independent director on the boards of companies, including Coca-Cola Hellenic, member of the

Advisory Board EMEA, Credit Suisse and Senior advisor Frigoglass, and Coca-Cola beverages. He has also served in various roles on nonprofit boards and committees, including as trustee of Thunderbird Global Management University and the American Community School, Beirut; advisory board member of the Churchill Archives Center at Cambridge University; member, for ten years, of the Dean's Council at the John F Kennedy School of Government, Harvard; and board member of American Near East Refugee Aid (ANERA).

Samir currently lives in Santa Monica with his wife Abla, and near their two grown-up children and their grandchildren.